iPhone Photography Focusing On Macro

A technical look at iPhone photography with tips on taking macro images.

By **Greg McMillan**

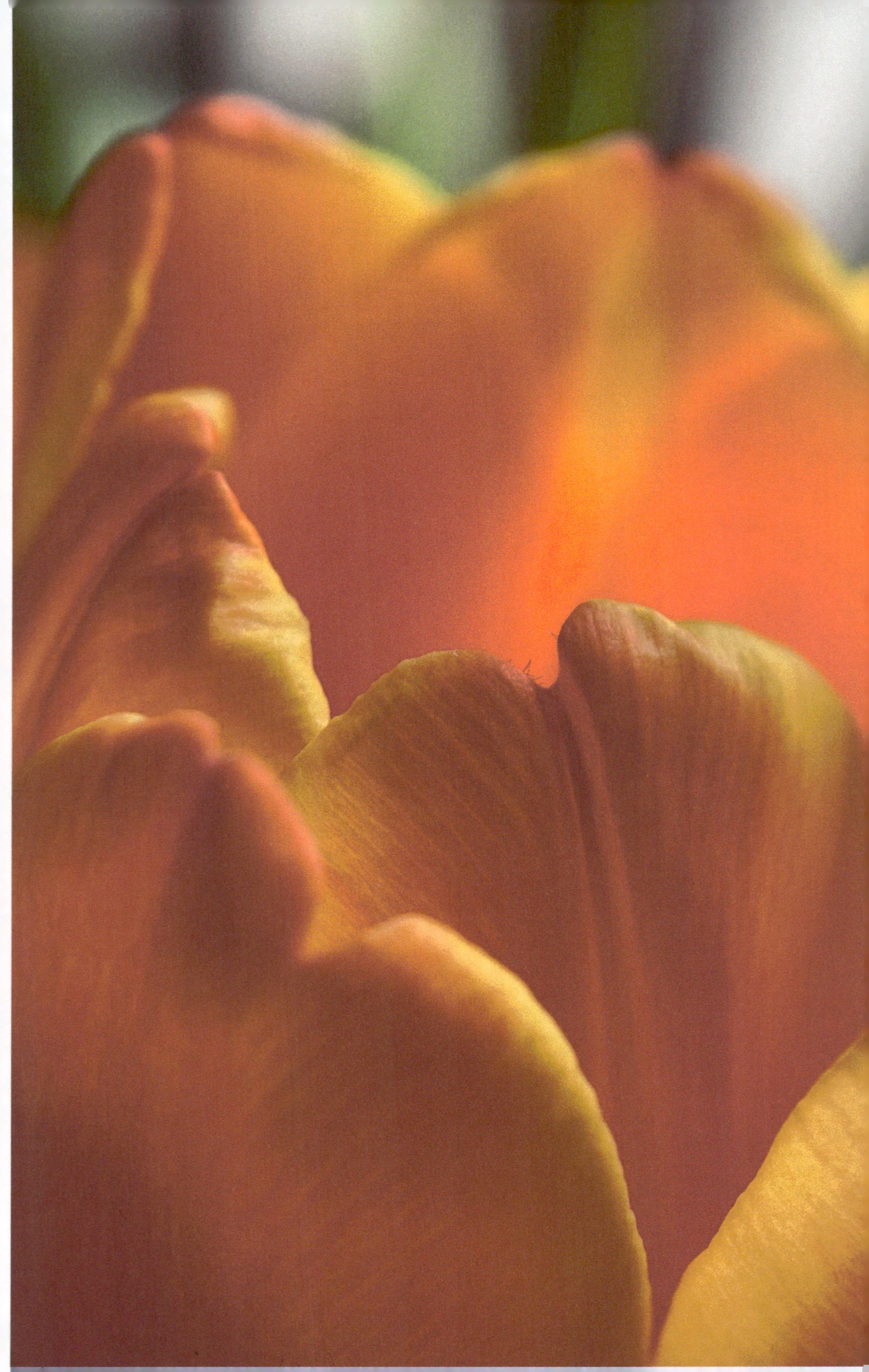

Greg McMillan
greg@mcmillan.photos
https://mcmillan.photos

iPhone Photography Focusing On Macro is an independent publication and has not been authorized, sponsored, or otherwise approved by Apple Inc.

First published in 2024 by McMillan Media

Foreword by Shayne Mostyn

ISBN: 987-1-9994876-2-1 (electronic version)
ISBN: 987-1-9994876-3-8 (print version)

Apple, iPhone, iPad, Mac, and iMac are trademarks of Apple Inc.

Adobe, Lightroom and Lightroom Mobile are either registered trademarks or trademarks of Adobe in the United States and/or other countries.

Any and all other applications mentioned in this publication are trademarks of their respective developers.

Table of Contents

Foreword

I first came across Greg "Macro" McMillan not long after I started my mobile photography YouTube channel. He reached out to me to ask if I would come onto his Podcast. At the time, I really had no idea who he was and his request got lost in the many requests I was receiving at the time. He persisted in contacting me and I'm very glad he was persistent because I now have a great mate on the other side of the globe who I really enjoy spending time with, albeit, online when we host my channel's live streams every two weeks. We banter like brothers and I will always be grateful for his friendship.

Soon enough, I found him to be my "go-to guy" when it came to macro photography with an iPhone. Here I was pushing the limits of a phone camera sensor to capture the night sky and there was Greg, pushing the limits of these same cameras up close and personal with macro photography. I have always been impressed with his passion for macro, his knowledge of the subject, and his humility. I found myself closing my mouth and opening my ears when Greg spoke about macro photography.

I was truly humbled when Greg asked me to write the foreword for this book. The book has been a long time coming and I have shared the highs and lows with Greg, as he had to deal with all sorts of obstacles that come with printing a book during a global pandemic. I'm glad he also decided to release it in an electronic form, it gets this knowledge into the reader's hands so much faster.

This book is like an unpacking of Greg's knowledge and passion for iPhone macro photography. This type of photography on an iPhone is one of the more difficult genres of photography to master. Greg makes it very easy to understand and enjoyable to learn.

He writes about the apps, the tools, and the skillsets to capture the smallest things in the world and make them larger than life. He shows examples and screenshots to help you along the way. What's in the book is the same as what you will see on your iPhone. The photos that Greg has chosen to include in this book are a testament to his abilities as an iPhone macro photographer.

The reader should be excited to delve into this book. You are about to do things with your iPhone that you didn't know were possible.

Shayne Mostyn

Creator

Shayne Mostyn - Mobile Photography YouTube Channel.

Introduction

When I started my journey in photography, I never dreamed I would do macro work, much less use a phone to take pictures. I'm old enough to have started my journey using film, 110 film in fact. Wow, that sure dates me, doesn't it? However, I never got serious about photography until about 20 years ago, and by serious I don't mean doing it professionally, I just mean I wanted to learn more about it and improve my photos. I've never had the desire to sell my work. If someone wishes to buy a print, I'm always thankful for the fact that they think enough of it to want one on their wall.

In 2000, I bought a Canon Rebel XS 35mm SLR camera and, for the most part, was somewhat picky with what I shot. Of course, there was no way of knowing how the photos turned out until I got the prints back. But I generally worked on improving composition more than anything.

Three years later, the Rebel line became available as a digital offering, and being the tech geek that I am, I just had to get one. This began a whole new chapter in my photographic life. My progression escalated exponentially with all the new tools that were readily available to me, from the ability to capture as many photos as I wanted to the ever-increasing resources on the internet for learning all I could.

Fast forward to the age of the smartphone. When the iPhone was first released in 2007, I was quite resistant to give it a look. I was very much a BlackBerry fan and did not like Steve Jobs' concept of the closed ecosystem that was Apple. By then I had upgraded my DSLR to a newer Rebel model and would soon move to a Canon

60D, so taking photos with a phone had not really interested me… yet.

When the iPhone 4 came out, things started to change for me. I saw the image quality available from that phone and I immediately started to think twice about Apple and pay more attention to what they were all about. I began to realize that Apple's business model made sense. By then, Jobs had fallen ill, and unfortunately wasn't around much longer.

Instagram had become a thing and the mobile photography movement was in full force. I had taken a few photos with my BlackBerry but the difference between that and the iPhone was like night and day. With the release of the iPhone 4s in October 2011, I found myself ready to make the move to Apple. I could immediately see the benefits of shooting with an iPhone - shoot, edit and share, all from the same device. The simplicity of it was infectious and I found myself doing a 366 project on Instagram for 2012.

I bought a new iPhone every two years which kept me on the "s" cycle, that is until what was to be the 7s came out as the 8, 8 Plus and X (pronounced "10"). I opted for the plus sized version of the 8 because the price difference for the X wasn't, in my opinion, justifiable. However, the Xs released the following year was everything I expected to see with the X, so for the first time, I upgraded to the larger Xs Max after just one year.

When I began writing this book, I still had the Xs Max and it served as a companion to my 12 Pro Max. As time passed I upgraded to the 14 Pro Max, then eventually to the 15 Pro Max and sold the Xs Max. The image quality of the 15 Pro Max is out-of-this-world good.

I wanted to give you a little history about how I got to where I am today but this book isn't about that, it's about a specific genre of iPhone photography - macro. Macro photography, by definition, is when the image on the sensor or film is equal to or greater than life size. The ability to capture something "larger than life" in any camera is certainly nothing new but being able to do it with an iPhone has only been possible for a few years.

As mentioned earlier, I never thought I would do macro photography with a phone. In fact, I resisted it emphatically because I refused to believe one should put lenses on a phone. That was reserved for DSLRs. Then one day, back when I had my iPhone 6s, I was in a local camera store talking shop with the owner and he asked if I had tried lenses on my iPhone. I said I had not and expressed how I had no desire to do so.

He showed me a kit of ProMaster clip-on lenses and was willing to let me take them home to try before I decided to purchase them. I tried a couple of them at the store right away - the wide angle and the macro - and admittedly I was hooked. Forget the free trial. I bought the set on the spot.

My favourite lens in that kit was the macro because, as you'll read later in this book, macro photography takes you into a whole new photographic experience. It turns an already big world into something much bigger because macro work makes the smallest things look massive.

Throughout this book, we will delve into how the iPhone camera works to help you make the most of it, and if you haven't tried macro photography before, I hope this book will show you how much fun it can be. I started writing this book in the midst of the pandemic, and thanks to the ability to shoot macro, I definitely had something to write about. Thank you for joining me on this amazing journey through the following pages of a whole new world.

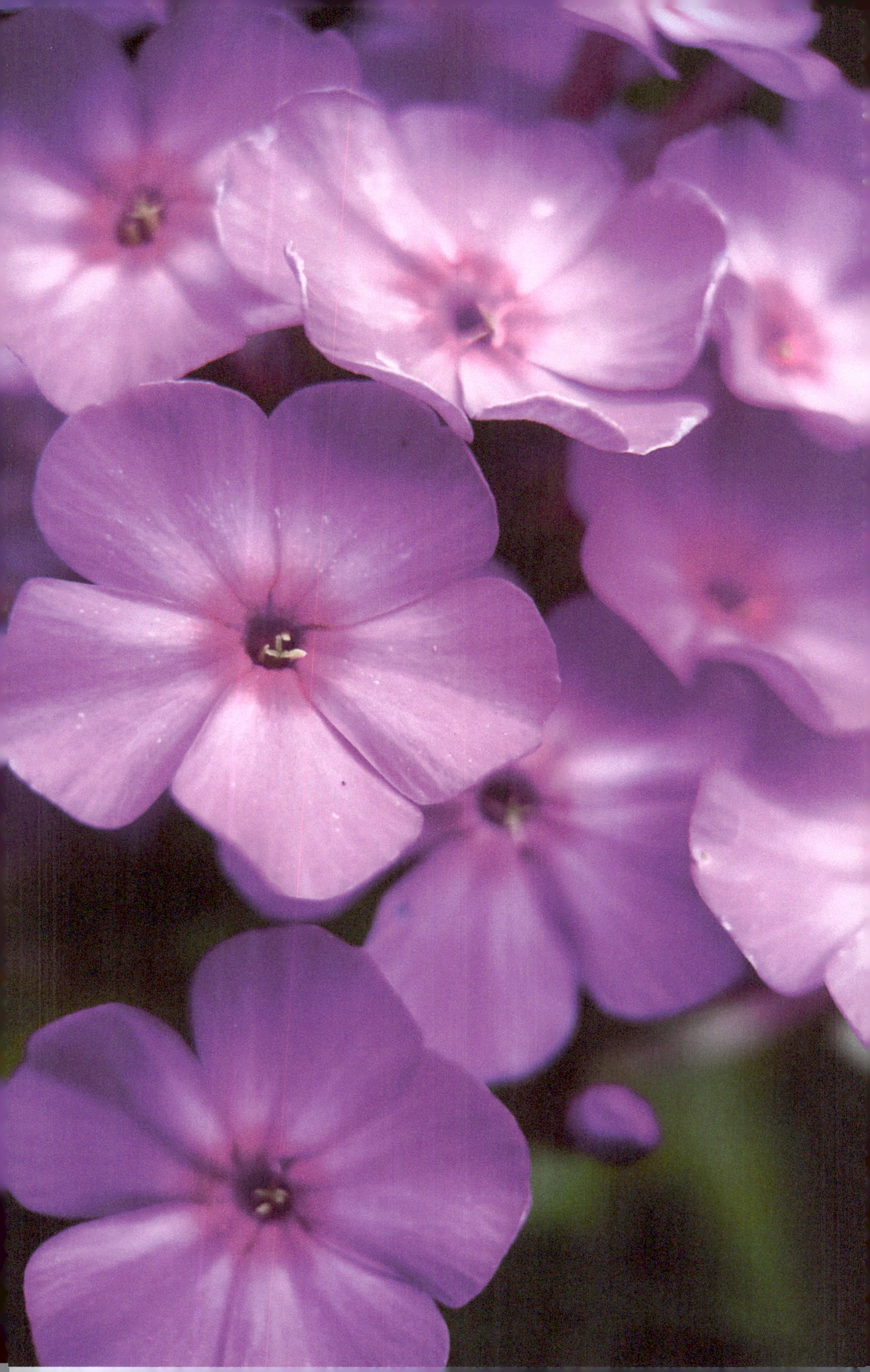

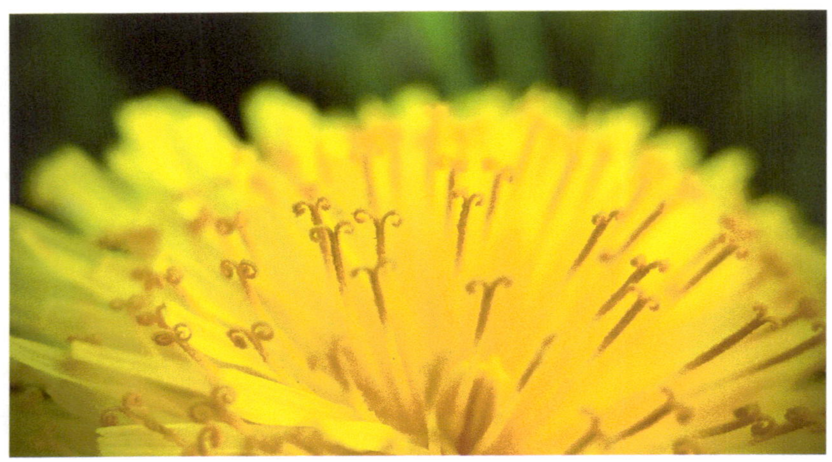

Chapter 1 - Gear

Doing macro photography successfully with an iPhone requires a couple of things in particular: a lens and a good third-party camera app. But why would you need a third-party camera app when the iPhone already has a great Camera app built into the operating system? Well, as much as it is good, it's my opinion that it is equally flawed for some forms of this type of work.

Since the launch of the iPhone 7 Plus in September 2016, there has been the option to have an iPhone with a multi-camera system. The iPhone 11 brought us an Ultra Wide camera but it's ability for macro work without an additional lens began on the iPhone 13 Pro and Pro Max. For clarity in this book, I'll refer to what some folks call the "1x" camera as the Main camera, because that's what Apple calls it, and the "2, 3 or 5x" (if equipped) I'll call the Telephoto camera.

These cameras, the Main and the Telephoto, work independently of each other… sort of. The Main camera has always been fitted with optical image stabilization and a larger aperture than the Telephoto, which is why it always produces better image quality. When taking a telephoto shot in ample light, the Telephoto camera will perform as expected, but if the conditions are less than optimal, the Main camera actually zooms digitally while still giving you a full resolution image, and in every iPhone since the 6s, that's 12 megapixels, or 12 MP. Once the Main camera reaches a certain zoom range (in the case of the 7 Plus it was between 1.5x and 1.99x) the telephoto lens blends higher resolution imagery into the centre of the frame, something Apple calls "fusion". This gives sharper detail to avoid the muddy look of a digitally zoomed image. That's the best I can explain it but I'm sure it sounds very complicated.

MACRO WITHOUT A MACRO LENS

There are two ways to take macro photos without the aid of additional hardware, and that's with a Pro version of any iPhone beginning with the 13 Pro, or with a macro-enabled third-party app which I'll cover shortly. As I stated in the Introduction, I went from owning a 12 Pro Max to the 14 Pro Max, so I missed having the ability to shoot macro with the 13 Pro. My experience with the 14 Pro Max and now the 15 Pro Max has shown me that Apple has greatly improved the macro ability of the camera, both in image quality and in giving the image a more natural "macro" look.

The 14 Pro Max was quite user friendly in that you could get very close to your subject - in fact, the minimum focus distance in Macro Mode is 2cm - but I found there to be too much in focus, or simply put, the depth of field was too deep. This was improved with the 15 Pro Max as there is a little more fall off with regards to what is in focus, which is what I feel a macro should look like. Isolating your subject will yield the best results when doing macro with the iPhone's Camera app. The less clutter you have in the image, the better the image will look as you'll see in greater detail later in the book.

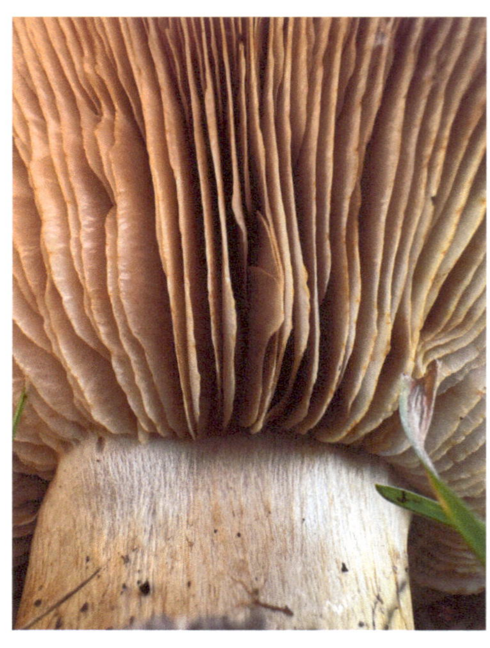

Shot in Macro Mode with iPhone 15 Pro Max.

The nice thing about the iPhone's natural macro ability is that you don't need to buy any lenses and carry that additional hardware in your pocket while out shooting. Apple has made it so easy to grab a macro shot by giving the camera the ability to automatically switch

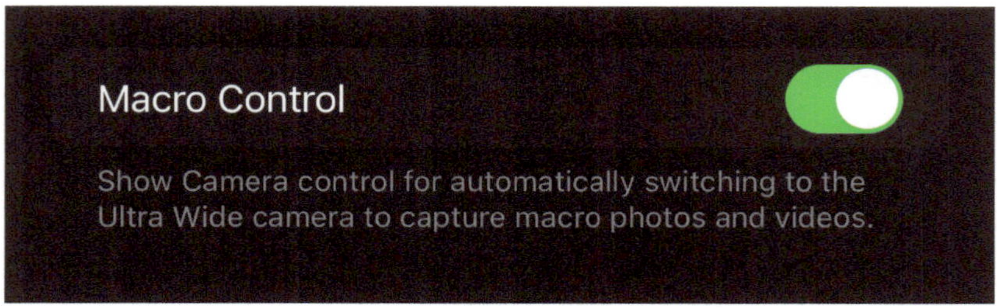

Macro Control turned on to enable Macro Mode.

to the Ultra Wide camera when you get too close for the Main camera to focus. This was at first a little bothersome to many a photographer out there but Apple fixed that by adding a toggle in the camera app's settings. In the Settings app under Camera, there is a toggle labelled Macro Control and with this turned off, the iPhone will not switch to the Ultra Wide camera and won't be able to take a macro photo. As you get closer to a subject you will just simply be too close to focus on anything.

With Macro Control turned on and when you get close enough to take a macro photo, the macro indicator appears in the corner of the viewfinder near the image preview thumbnail. This will be highlighted in yellow when Macro Mode is active and greyed out with a line through it when you are close to something but Macro Mode is not active. When you see the inactive icon you can tap it to force the camera into Macro Mode rather than wait for it to happen automatically. Also in the Camera settings under Preserve Settings there is another Macro Control toggle that, like any other preserved setting, can remember whether or not you have Macro Mode set to be on automatically or leave it off.

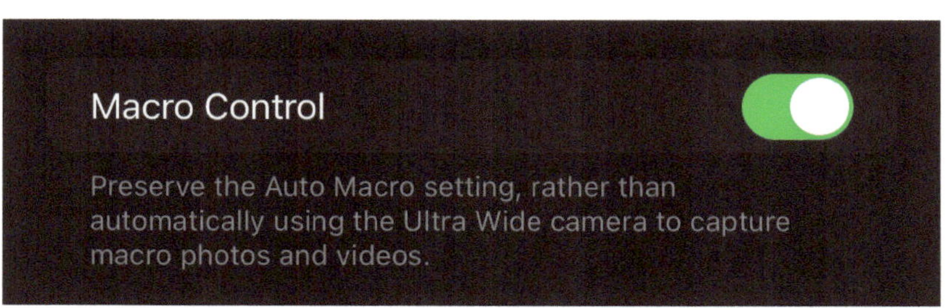

This setting sets the iPhone to remember your Macro Mode setting.

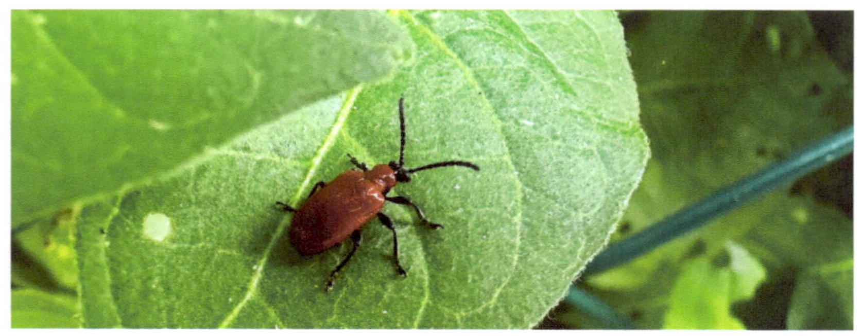

iPhone 14 Pro Max taken in Macro Mode.

MACRO WITH ACCESSORY LENSES

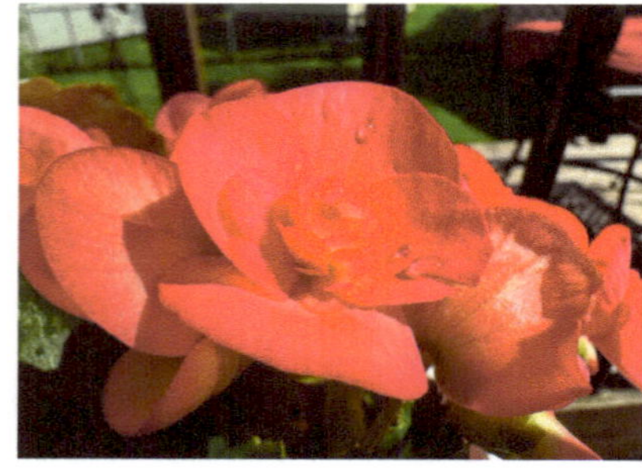

Shot without add-on lens.

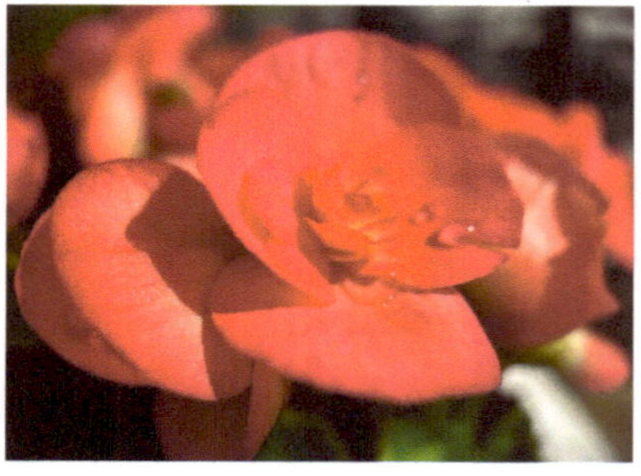

Shot with add-on lens.

To achieve the best macro photography results with an iPhone, you need to invest in a quality macro lens attachment. These can be affixed via a clip or mounted to a case. Olloclip was one of the most popular clip-on lenses on the market in the early days. Sadly, the global pandemic put Olloclip on hiatus indefinitely. However, at the time of this book publication, their website is still running, albeit with no e-commerce so I doubt they'll be back. The clip-on style can be tricky to align directly over the lens at the optimal distance over the camera to achieve the best results. Incorrect positioning could result in blurred edges of the frame, darkening on the edges (vignetting) and difficulty focussing.

The best way to use lenses is with a case, like the ones that work with Reeflex, Sandmarc, ShiftCam and Moment to name a few. The case mounted lens effortlessly aligns perfectly centred at the right distance from the camera for the best optics.

Moment uses a bayonet style mount where you line up the lens to the mount opening and give it a quarter turn to lock it in. The quality of glass used in Moment lenses is pretty good, but I do prefer a thread mounting system like those found on ShiftCam and Reeflex.

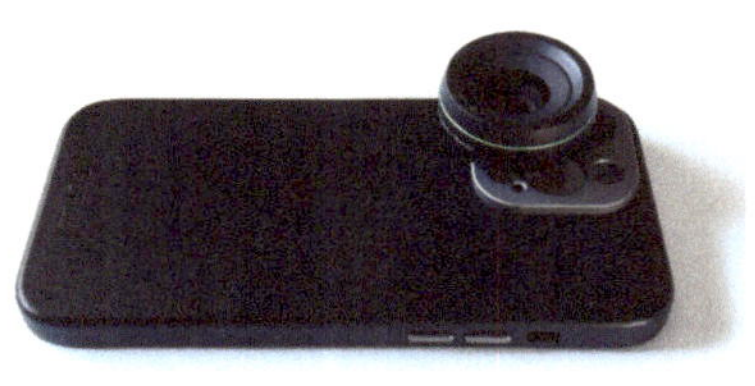

Reeflex Case with a G-Series Macro Lens.

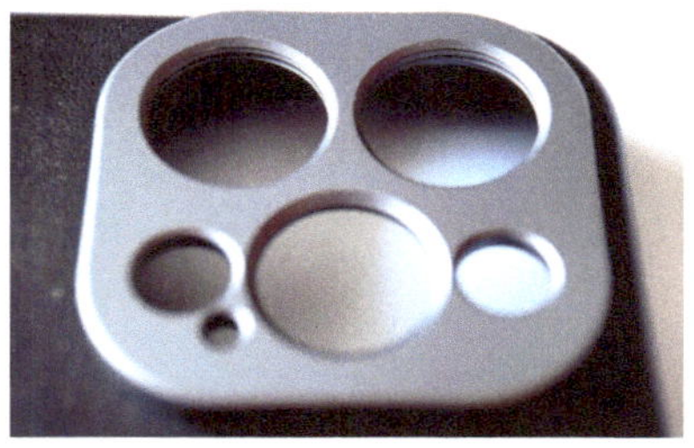

Reeflex 17mm Thread Mount.

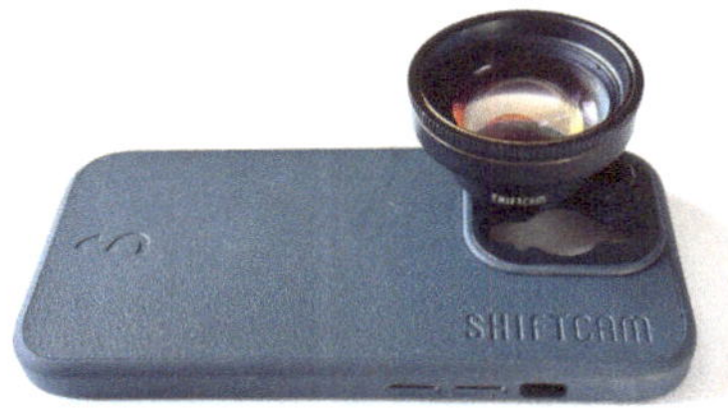

ShiftCam Case with Macro Lens.

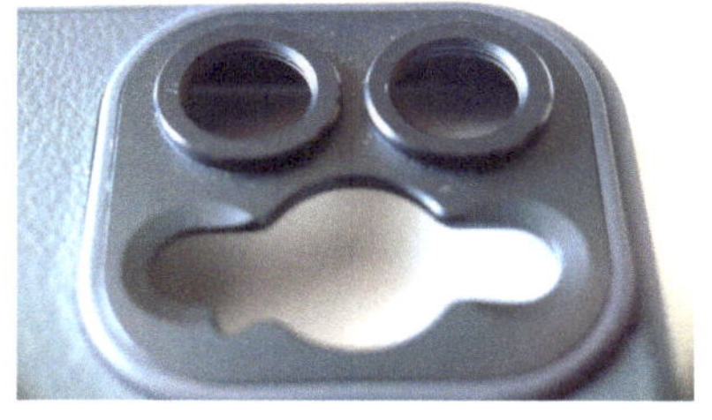

ShiftCam 12mm Thread Mount.

Mike James, from Smartphone Photography Training in Australia (you should check him out, he's amazing) was once an ambassador for an Australian company called Struman Optics. While watching one of Mike's YouTube videos, I was taken aback to see him combining the manual focus of the Struman Optics Cinematic Macro Lens and the focus peaking feature in the Lightroom Mobile app. I had talked on my podcast about writing this book and since Mike is a listener, he arranged for Struman Optics to send me a new macro lens to review. It is everything I hoped it would be with edge to edge sharpness and pristine image quality on my iPhone 12 Pro Max. This lens is a game-changer when it comes to doing macro photography with an iPhone. Unlike the fixed focal distance of other macro lenses, the focus ring provides creative and practical versatility.

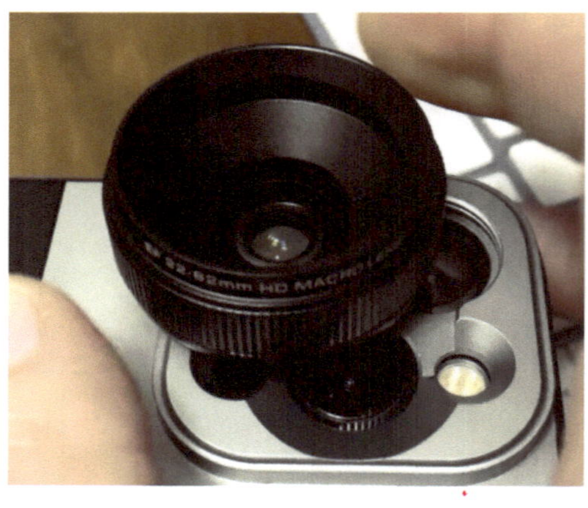

Struman Optics 22-82mm Cinematic Macro with 17mm Thread Mount and focus ring.

The depth of field is still fairly small with this lens, but when you set both the camera focus and the lens at maximum distance, you do have a deeper depth of field, which is quite useful for things like insects where you can get most, if not all of the bug in sharp focus.

I will be including some content related to the Struman lens later in the book when I write about Shooting Techniques.

I have also had the pleasure to get acquainted with the guys behind the Reeflex Pro Camera app who provided their Long Range

Macro lens and a Telephoto. Those lenses were their older generation products and they have since released the new G-Series lenses that you can see pictured on the previous page. Additionally, thanks to another Aussie friend, Shayne Mostyn, I have also acquired a set of lenses by ShiftCam. I now carry with me any number of lenses from any of these manufacturers whenever I go out shooting, They are all amazing products and love the results I get from them.

Most of the content going forward in the book will relate to shooting with an accessory lens but there may be times when I'll include images shot in Macro Mode.

THIRD PARTY CAMERA APPS

Third-party apps allow you to manually select the camera you want to shoot with. This eliminates the problem of trying to use the Telephoto (for those times when you want to get extra close) and having the iPhone attempt to utilize the Main camera due to the lack of good lighting.

Like the lenses, there are plenty of choices when it comes to camera apps. I have somewhere between 15-20 of these apps on my iPhone right now, but most of them are there because I do a podcast about iPhone photography and sometimes I need to have them installed so I can talk about them. When recommending camera apps, my shortlist of the best ones on the market are: Moment (another company who makes a camera app as well as lenses), ProCamera, Camera M, CameraPixels, Halide MkII and my app of choice, Reeflex. There are dozens of camera apps but these are, in my opinion, some of the best camera apps available.

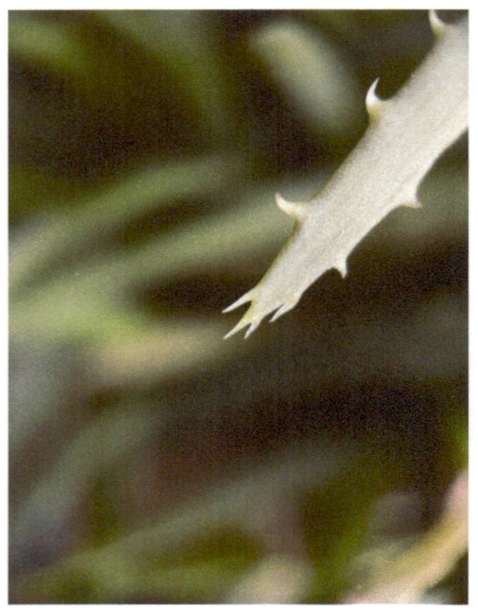

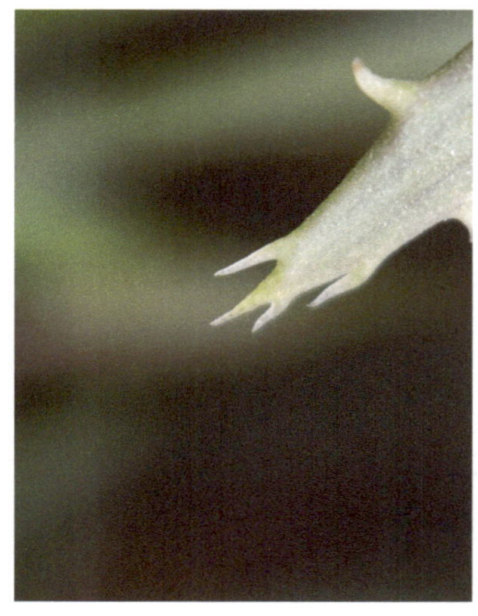

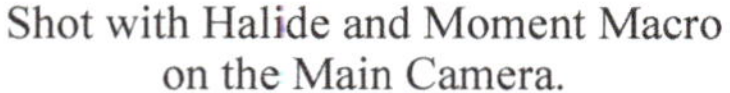

Shot with Halide and Moment Macro on the Main Camera.

Shot with Halide and Moment Macro on the Telephoto Camera.

I like Reeflex because it has a well-designed, intuitive interface, and like me, the developers are very enthusiastic about photography. There are some cool features in Reeflex that I'll be covering in various places throughout this book because they are very helpful when doing macro work. Other apps may indeed have the same features, but Reeflex was my app of choice at the time of writing this book.

Halide has a macro mode that is fairly effective because it utilizes the image quality of the Main camera and performs image upscaling to improve the quality of the final output. Halide's macro ability could put it in the category of shooting without a lens, but the fact that it can also be used with a lens warrants its presence in this section. In Halide, if you are shooting RAW or ProRAW with the JPG, you get the full resolution DNG file included with the upscaled, full resolution compressed file. It isn't the macro version, just the full

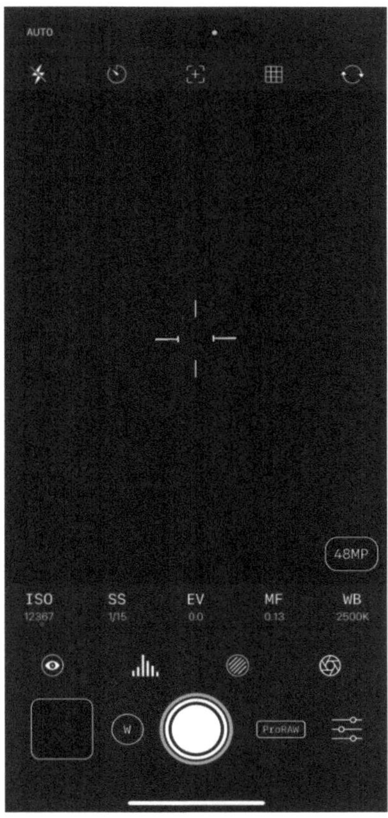

The Reeflex Pro Camera app.

image you would get from the Main camera as if you weren't using the Macro Mode.

I tested Halide's Macro Mode and compared it to The Apple Camera app zoomed in and I found Halide Macro to be much better in quality thanks to the upscaling. I should note that this was before I had an iPhone with Macro Mode built in. I showed some sample photos in episode 47 of The iPhoneography Podcast, which is on YouTube. Scan the QR code to watch that segment on your computer or smartphone. Halide's Macro Mode is accessed by tapping the "AF" icon on the left side below the viewfinder. When you tap it, the AF icon will slide to the right side of the screen and a tulip icon will take its place. Tap the tulip icon to enter Macro Mode and the tulip will slide to the right side. Above the tulip you will see another icon that indicates the zoom factor of the camera. You can tap the screen to use Auto Focus in Halide Macro or slide the scale above the shutter button

Scan the QR code to watch the Halide Macro video on YouTube.

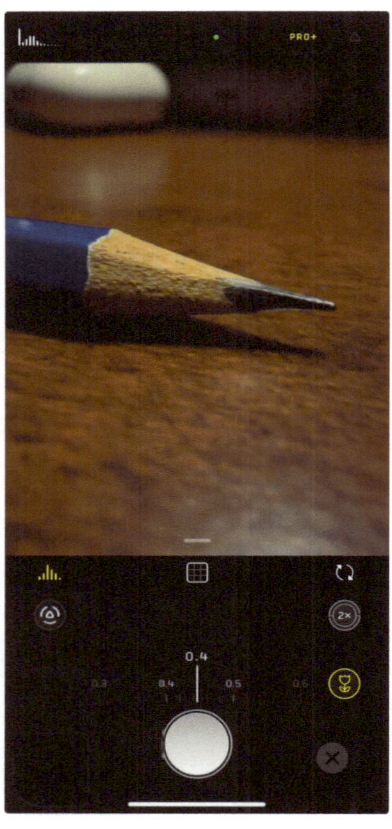

Macro Mode in Halide MkII.

to access finer manual focus. This is handy to apply the sharpness in just the right part of the frame.

In Halide's Macro Mode, you can utilize focus peaking. This is a colour visual overlay over the preview image letting you know exactly which part of the frame is in sharp focus. The focus peaking interface in Halide is upscaled so the green lines that appear along the edges of areas in sharp focus are thicker than normal. This can make it harder to determine exactly where that tack sharp focus is located.

Most third party camera apps will feature focus peaking, manual focus, manual camera selection, exposure controls for ISO and shutter speed, white balance and more. The flexibility of these apps make it worth using them for not just macro, but any form of iPhone photography.

HOLDING THINGS STEADY

Sometimes shooting macro can be painfully tricky if you have shaky hands. Resting the iPhone on or against something steady or tucking your elbows in against your body and exhaling your breath

as you press the shutter can help.
Also, be sure you don't squeeze
the phone tightly in your hand as
this will lead to shaking it.

ProCamera by Cocologics is a
3rd-party camera app equipped
with an anti-shake feature. It uses
the motion sensors in your iPhone
to delay the capture until the
iPhone is held steady based on the
motion sensitivity that you can set.

There are also some pieces of
gear that will help hold your
iPhone steady, including: tripods,
monopods, and gimbals. You don't

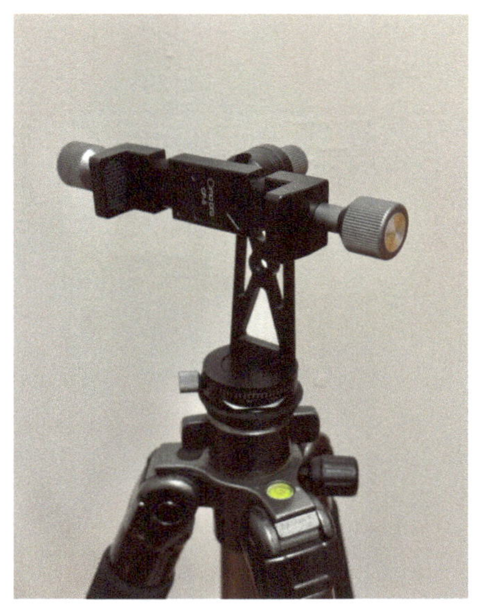

This iPhone mount has screw-down
clamps for a better grip on my phone.

need a full-sized tripod that would normally be used with a DSLR
because there are other great options available. An iPhone is light
compared to its larger, heavier counterparts so you could easily get
by with a GorillaPod. These little gems come in a variety sizes with
flexible legs that can hold your phone like a normal tripod or you can
wrap it around things like branches or railings to get close to your
subject.

Of course, you'll need a phone mount to attach to any type of
tripod head. These can be reasonably priced and popular brands
include Joby (the makers of the GorillaPod), Ulanzi and Manfrotto.
When purchasing a phone mount, consider having a built in Arca-
Swiss quick release mount that can slide into most tripod heads. A
cold shoe mount built into the top for additional accessories, and a
screw-down clamp instead of the spring-loaded options. You have

invested a lot of money in your iPhone and you don't want it falling off the tripod.

The reason you may want to use a tripod, beyond just wanting to hold your iPhone still, is so you can achieve good, sharp focus on your subject. Shooting macro with an iPhone offers a very shallow depth of field and the slightest movement is magnified when trying to compose.

A monopod may be a better solution than the tripod because it has one leg and offers more flexibility in moving your iPhone around your subject while maintaining some degree of stability. If you already have a tripod you can replicate this convenience by extending one of the legs. It should be noted too that when selecting a tripod, one with a ball head works best as it is much easier to manoeuvre.

I must admit, recent iPhones, especially the Pro models, the Main Camera has in-body-image-stabilization, or Sensor Shift Stabilization as Apple calls it. Instead of the lens providing the steadiness, the sensor itself adjusts thousands of times per second and I can say with assurance, this is generally better than using a gimbal.

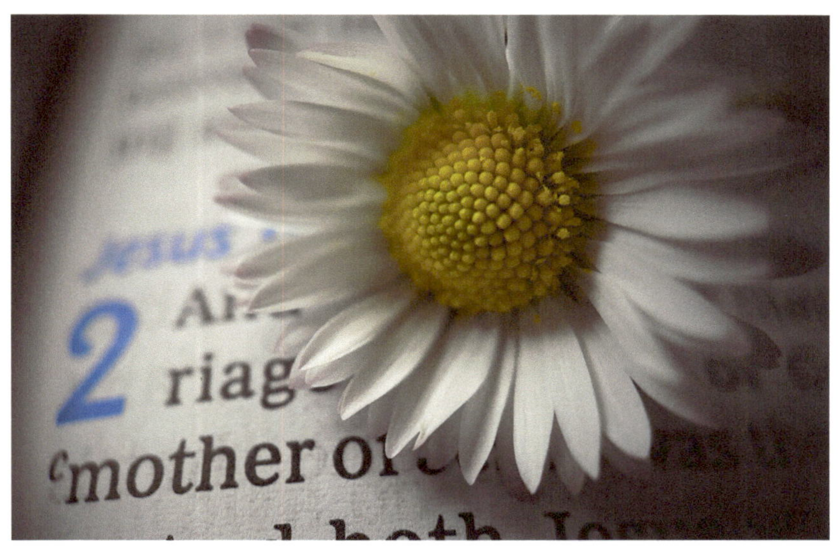

Chapter 2 - Exploring a Whole New World

THE TINIEST THINGS CAN BECOME SO LARGE

What I've discovered over the years is that macro photography takes you out of the "normal" world and presents you with something completely different. I think that's why I became such a fan of it the minute I tried it. A very smart woman, Meri Walker, once told me about how she immerses herself in her surroundings while doing photography. I was really amazed that she could do that because I find it difficult to be consciously aware of everything around me when my attention is directed at a viewfinder.

Nonetheless, viewing intricate details extremely close up is an amazing discovery and creative experience, viewing what is often the unseen world around us.

When the tiniest things become much bigger it's like stepping into another dimension. When I first picked up a camera all those years ago, my main passion was landscapes. Locating and finding an interesting composition of foreground, middle and background can be challenging. With macro, one of my favourite composition techniques is to fill the frame matching the photographic intention of showcasing the intricate details.

MACRO, ACCESSIBLE TO ALL

With macro photography, you don't even need to leave your home. There have been times when I feel the urge to create a photo, and whether it's because I couldn't get out or I just couldn't think of anywhere to go, I can grab my lens, attach it to my iPhone and start exploring my living room. The possibilities are endless for things to photograph. We have many house plants and a few trinkets on shelves that, although they're nice to look at, they would make boring

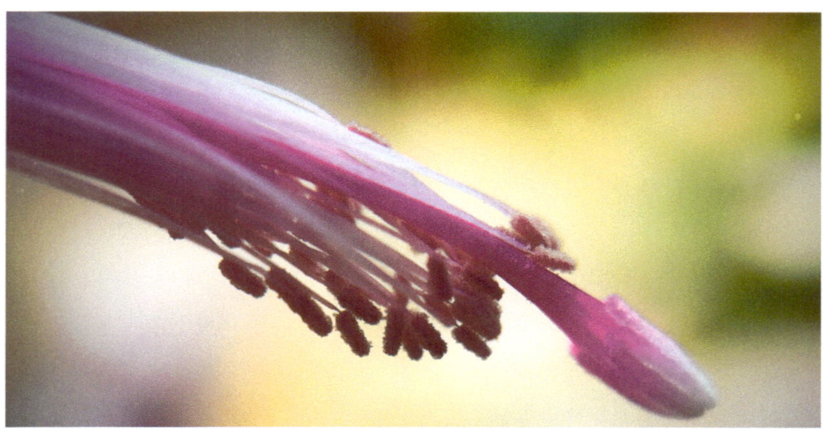

African Violet Stamen.

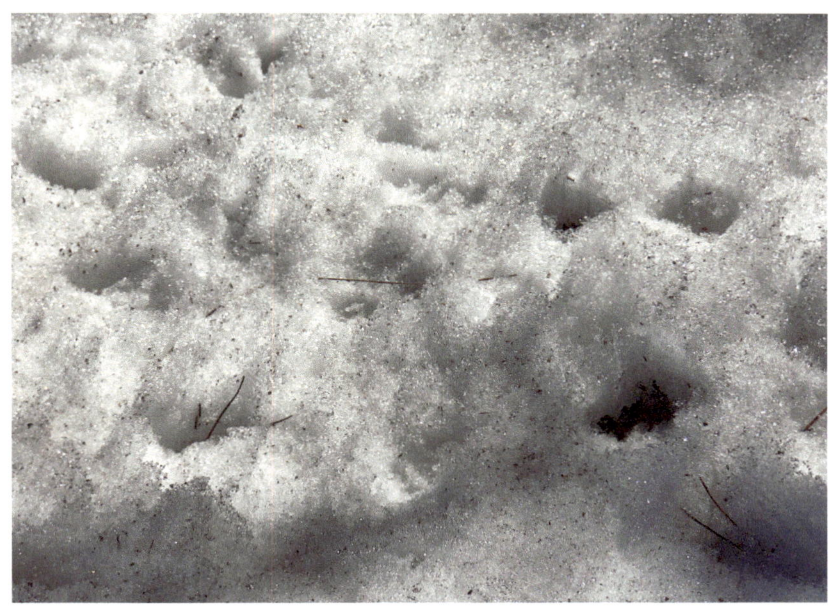

This is how we normally see melting snow.

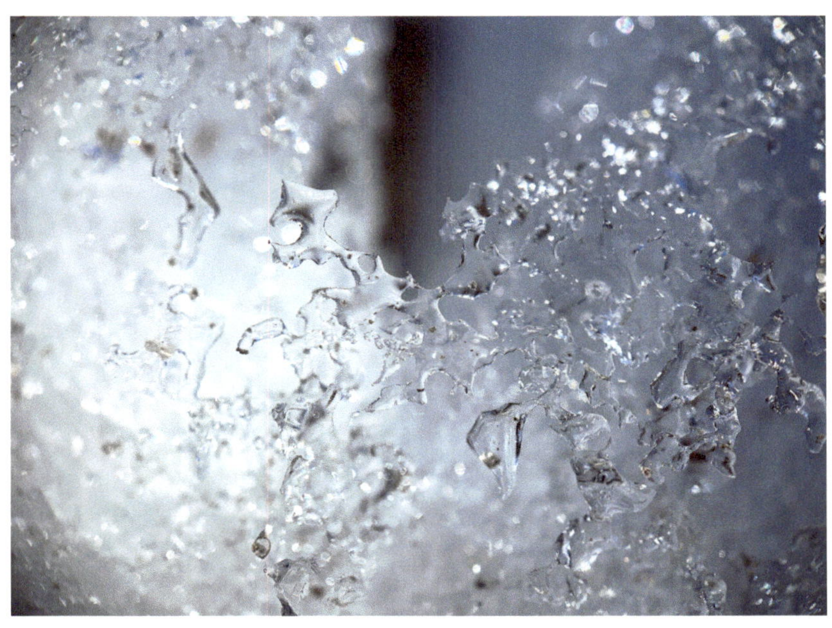

This is how you can explore melting snow
with a macro lens.

photos. Hone in on the stamen of an African Violet and you just bought yourself an easy fifteen minutes to waste. The next thing you know, you're capturing the texture of a doily or trying to create a portrait of porcelain figurine.

Staying home and getting lost in macro shooting is certainly not limited to indoors. If you have a garden or flower bed, there are plenty of opportunities there too. Take my example of the ant, for instance. We had a Rose of Sharon shrub in our back yard and when it was in full bloom during late summer, the ants and bees loved it. They're quick to move about, yes, but it's fun trying to predict where

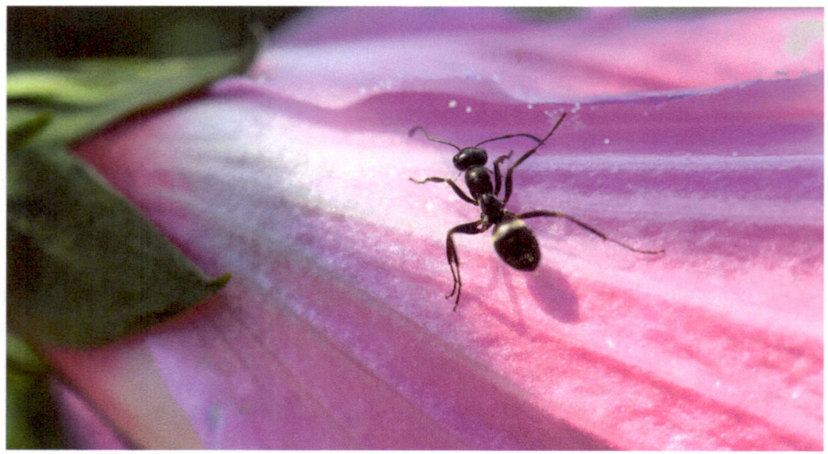

The Elusive Ant.

they might go next. One of my favourite shots of an ant was taken with my iPhone 6s with the clip-on macro lens that was part of the ProMaster kit mentioned earlier in the Introduction. On the Rose of Sharon shrub, the ant was frolicking about one of the blossoms when it went to the back side of it and out of sight. I kept the phone pointed at the flower, knowing it would either bolt down the stem or reappear on the front of a petal. As luck would have it, the ant didn't disappoint and came out from behind right at the bottom of the petal and I was able to capture it just before it darted up toward the stamen, and it was in perfect focus.

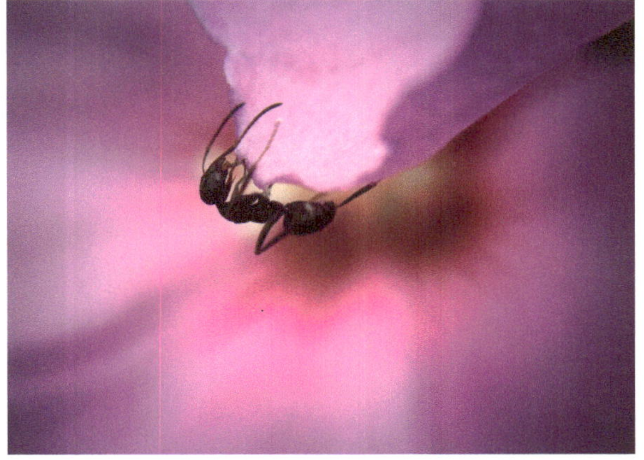

Chasing ants and bees.

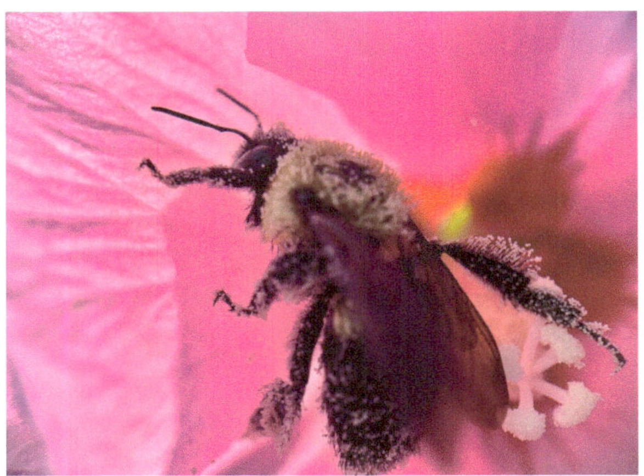

If you go for a walk in the woods, to a local park, or through the city streets, and plan to try macro photography, give yourself plenty of time because you can lose yourself in these settings too. Something to be remember, though, is to be aware of where you are and what you're shooting. If you're walking down the street and find some flowers you'd like to explore, make the determination about whether they're on private property or in public domain. The last thing you want is an angry property owner yelling at you to get off their lawn. A park or on a trail somewhere is a pretty safe place to practice without anyone bothering you.

Macro photography is an intimate form of the art. It's just you and your tiny subject, and unlike street photography, it's easy to see that you're capturing something very isolated from the rest of the world and that should put any onlookers at ease knowing they aren't going to be photographed. In fact, it may even prompt them to ask what you're shooting with the camera so close to your subject. It's a great conversation starter and an opportunity to let them into your new little world.

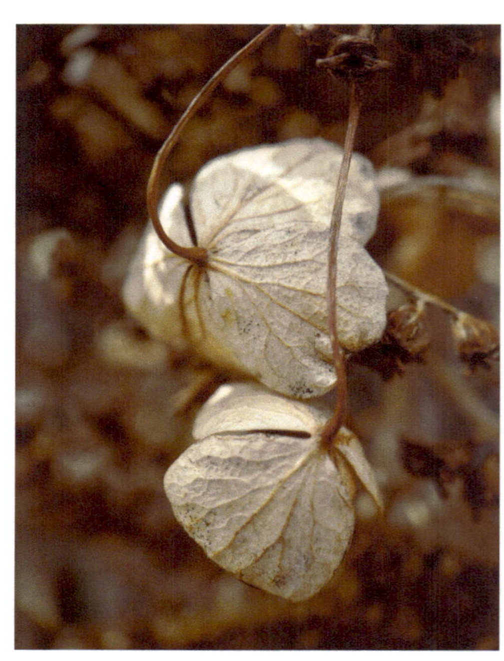

Taken from a sidewalk in front of someone's home.

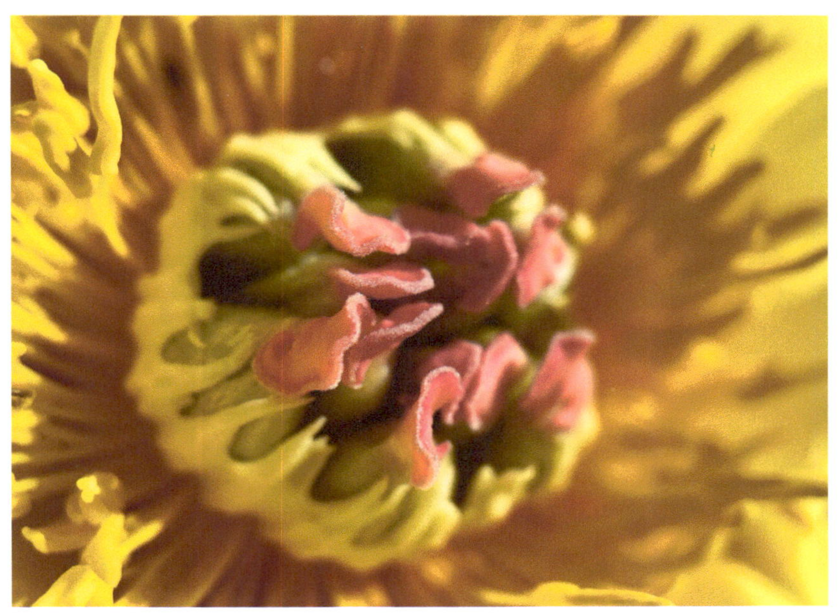

Chapter 3 - Working With Light

EXPLORING DIFFERENT LIGHTING SITUATIONS

In all my photography, I rarely use any form of artificial light to illuminate my subjects. Some will argue that natural light should not include any form of light created by humans, but my idea of natural light is light that occurs naturally in the environment you are in. If I take a photo of something on my desk at night, and I have a desk lamp on to light the room, that, to me, is natural light. Sure, sunlight or even moonlight is natural light in its purest form, but the point I'm making is that when I say "natural light" I mean I'm not using any type of photography related equipment to purposefully light a subject.

HARSH, MIDDAY SUNLIGHT

Full sun can introduce harsh shadows on your subject. Even the iPhone itself can cast a shadow. You can manage this by changing your approach angle or controlling the direction and/or intensity of light bouncing light back onto your subject using a mirror or white board.

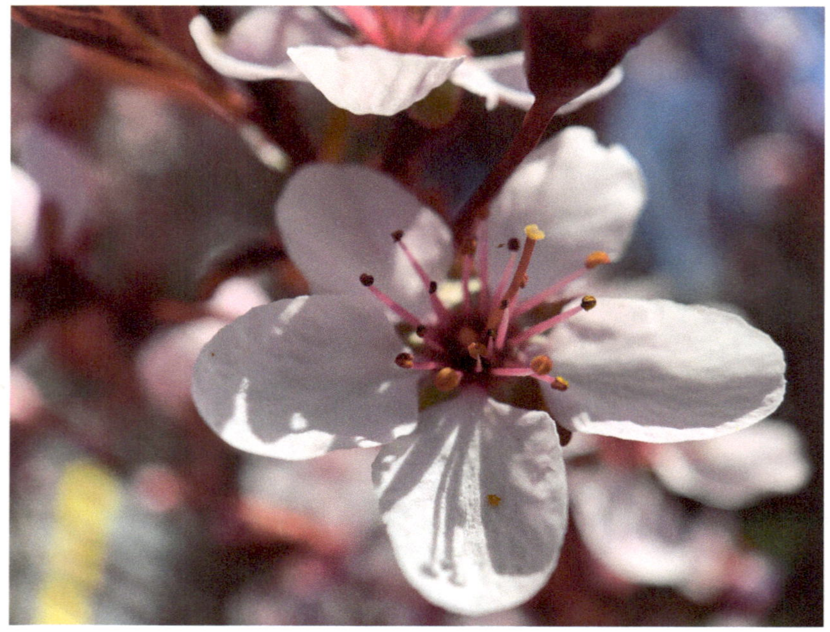

Harsh, midday sunlight.

Apart from stunning silhouette opportunities, the main advantage of full sun is a faster shutter speed to freeze the subject and avoid both camera and subject movement. A recent example was shooting the blossoms on our purple leaf sand cherry bush. Getting in close to capture a sharp photo of these very small flowers in full frame requires good lighting, as the slightest breeze will flutter it back and forth.

Having your subject shaded on a sunlit day can have its advantages too. For instance, in the case of a blossom, you may have the opportunity to take a photo of it in some shade while the sun lights up the

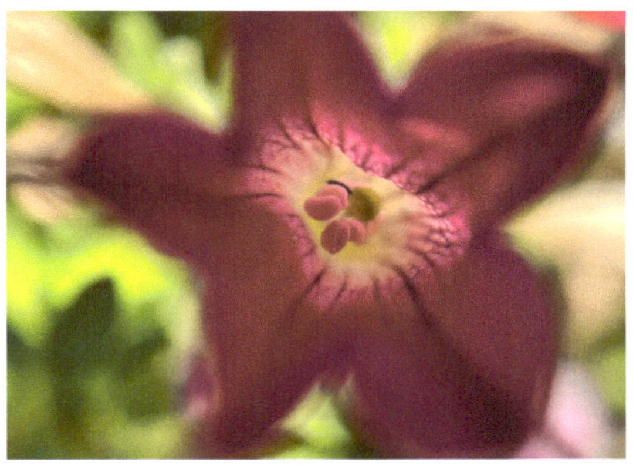

Shaded flower and sunlit background.

background. The camera will expose for wherever you tap to focus but the background will be fine because the iPhone has such an incredible ability to capture a large range of exposure latitude. It's hard to say how this will work for you since there are endless

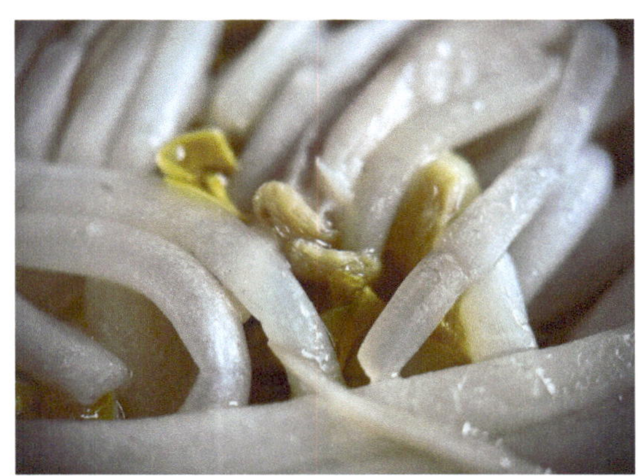

Chow Mien lit by a window.

scenarios possible, but it's something to consider when shooting on a sunny day.

Overcast skies are ideal for macro photography outdoors, while shooting in full shade provides the same diffused even light as an overcast day. The same could be said for indoor work where, if it's sunny out, there should be ample light for your macro shots as long as the sun isn't casting harsh light through a window and onto your subject. Shooting in full shade will give you the same diffused light as an overcast day, so if you're able to explore a shaded area, that too will make it easier to approach your subject.

THE DIFFUSER

Some macro lenses come with a diffuser that you press on over the front of the lens, like a lens hood used on traditional camera lenses. The diffuser is semi-transparent, like frosted glass except it's made of plastic. It protrudes out from the front of the lens and provides diffused light even in bright sunlight. If my subject is small enough, and isn't alive and moving about like an ant, the diffuser can be used to hold it still. The best example is when you are shooting a small flower or leaf on a day where there is even the slightest breeze, the diffuser covers and surrounds the part you're trying to capture and holds it still while the rest of the plant is moving with the wind. Your iPhone will have a certain range of focus that will fall somewhere between the outer

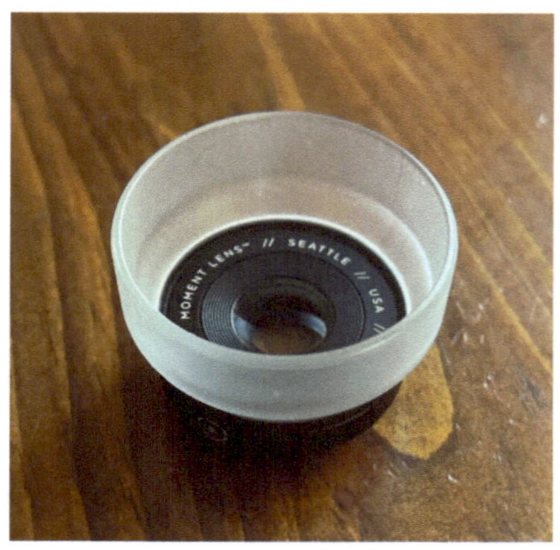

The Moment diffuser.

rim of the diffuser and wherever the minimum focus distance is, depending on which iPhone you have, so even though your subject is inside the diffusor, you can still obtain sharp focus.

SIDE AND BACK LIGHT

I have covered bright sunlight and diffused light, but there are a couple of other ways of using light that are worth exploring. The first one is side lighting. This is when your subject is lit from one side or the other which can be very useful

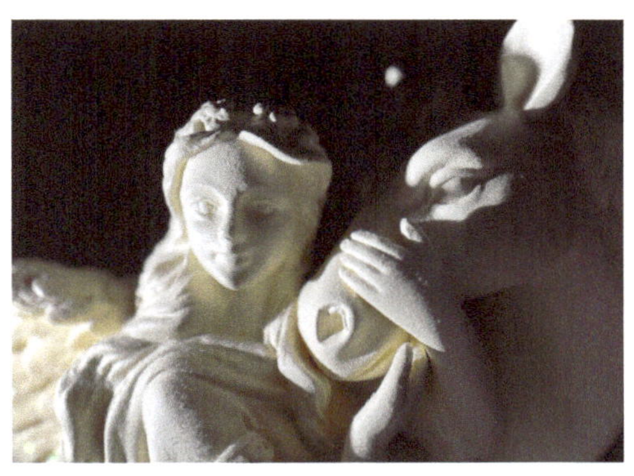

A figurine with side light.

in giving your image a nice artistic look. Whether your light source is from the sun or you use some artificial source of light, like a flashlight for example, side light can make anything more interesting

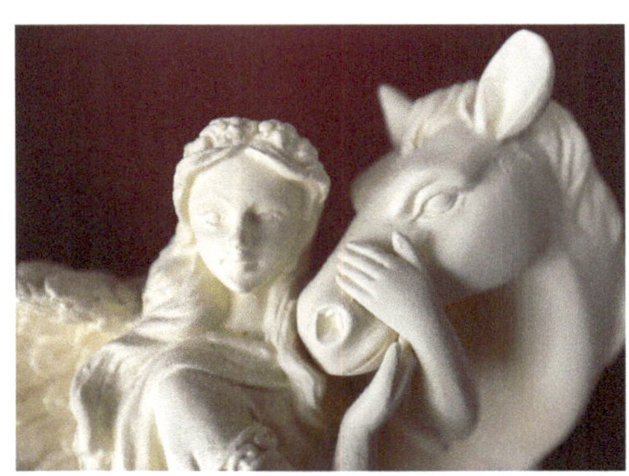

A figurine with diffused light.

because it can give it a sense of depth. Try shooting a small figurine - treat it like a portrait - while lighting it from the side and see how it changes the dynamics of the image when compared to, say, diffused light. Using some gear that would normally be reserved for other types of work besides macro could include reflectors or diffusers that are often used for portraiture. This offers the ability to point light in any direction, and in this case, from the side. A reflector could push more direct, harsh side lighting and diffused light.

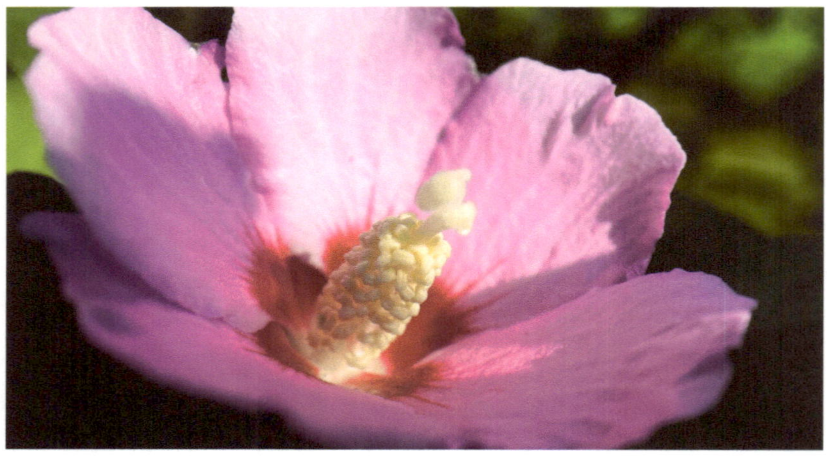

Rose of Sharon with side lighting.

Macro shots of flowers that are lit from the side will create lovely shadows cast by the petals or stamen, and because you're capturing it from such a close distance, this type of light will really enhance the texture of the petals or leaves. Some petals, depending on their physical

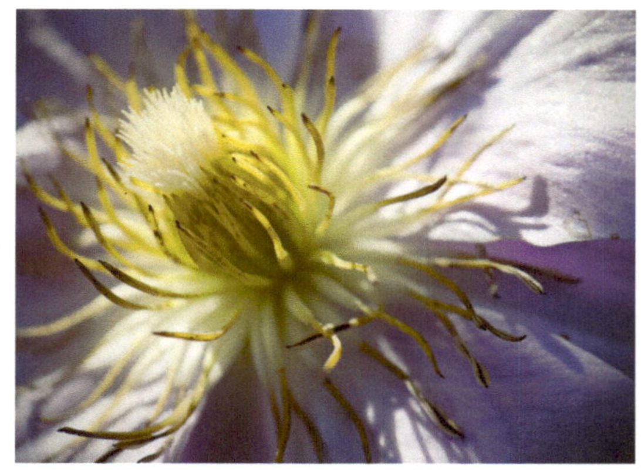

Clematis with side lighting.

properties, may even sparkle in the light which is something we just wouldn't see otherwise. Side light from the sun would generally be achieved during the early to mid-morning or late afternoon to evening hours. Coincidentally, I find these times to be better for any type of photography outdoors because when the sun is lower in the sky, it casts a warmer tone to everything.

The other method of lighting a subject is using backlight. This can be achieved by using the sun or any type of tool you can imagine, from a flashlight to a candle. Flowers shot with the sun behind them offer an opaque colour palette. If it's a delicate bloom, shadows from the sepal or other blooms that may be between it and the sun will appear on its petals. I realize I use flowers a lot in my examples, but that's what I enjoy shooting most with my macro lens.

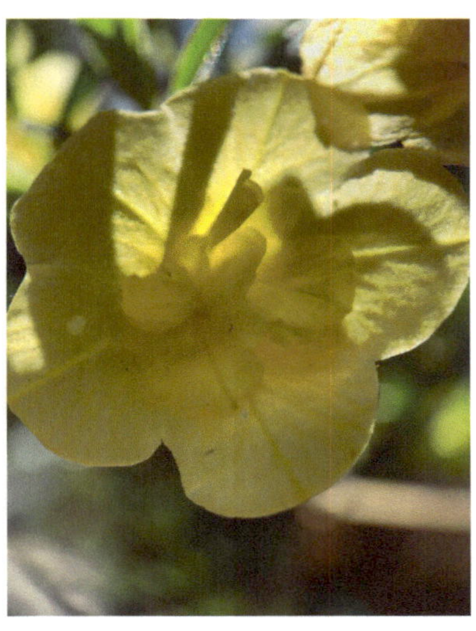

A yellow bloom lit from behind.

USE THE FLASH? NO WAY!

There's a question that may be burning in your mind right now when talking about the different forms of lighting, and that is, "Why not use the flash on the iPhone?" The flash produces a burst of light from the same direction as the camera, and often produces a flat looking image. Additionally, if you are using a lens attachment, it will either completely or partially block the light.

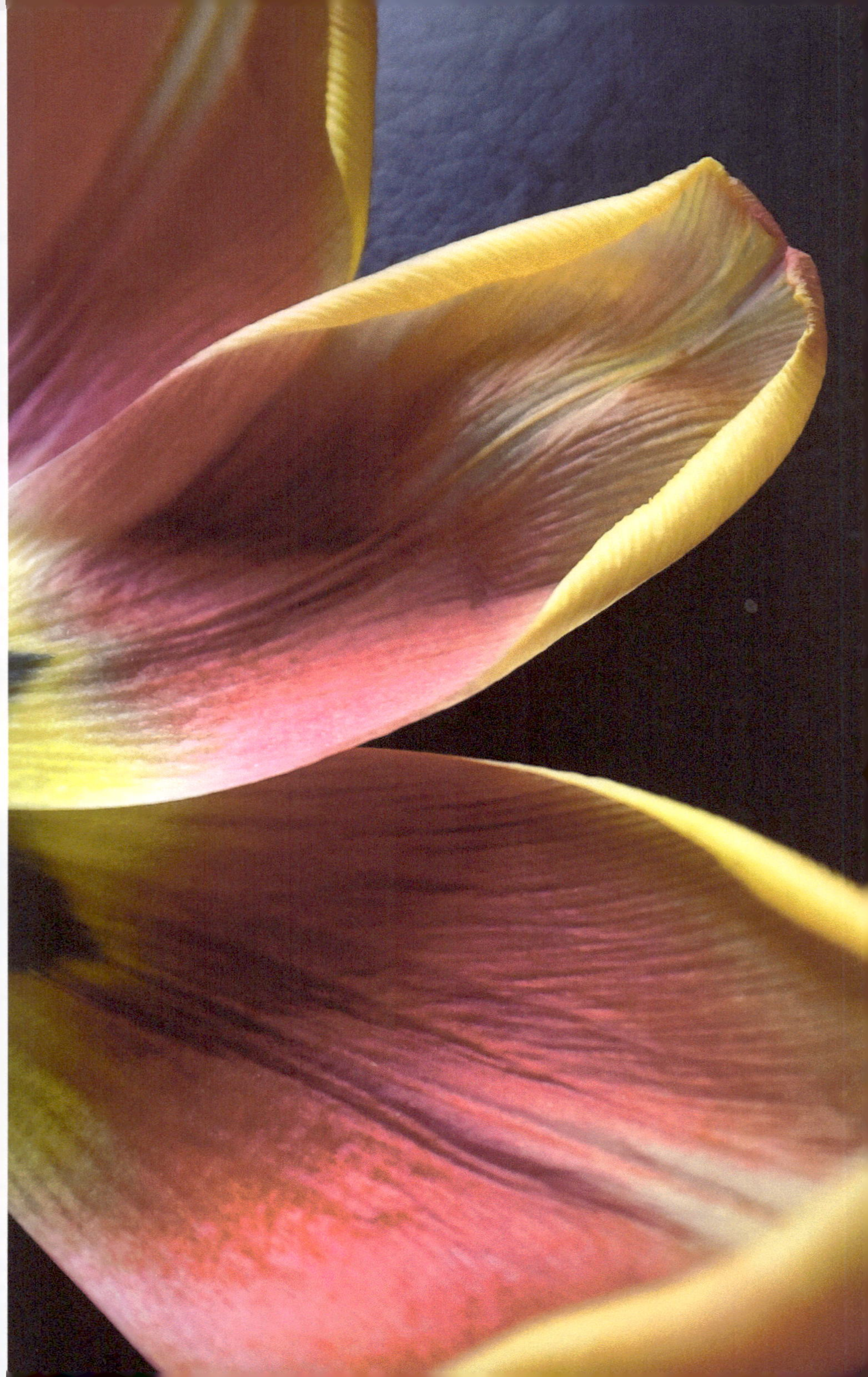

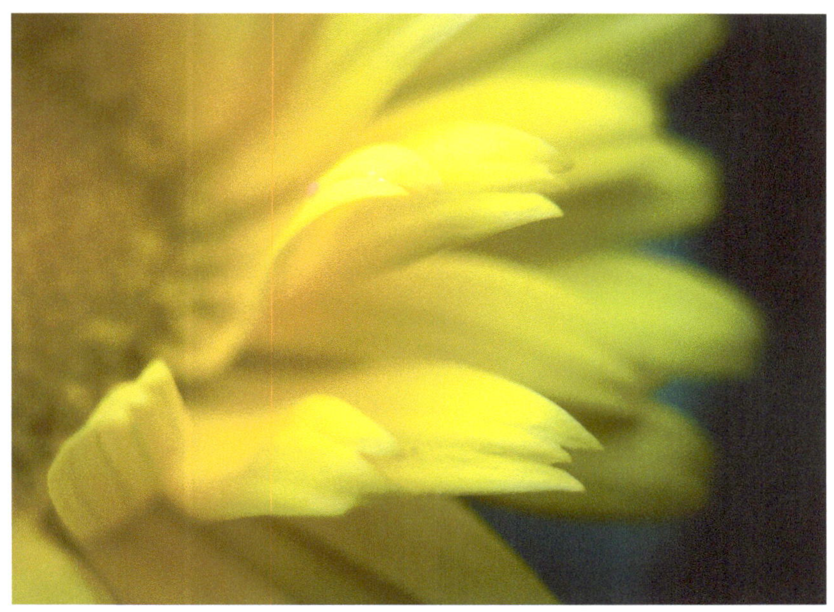

Chapter 4 - Flowers and Plants

FLOWERS

I'm sure it's no secret - I like shooting flowers with my macro lens because they're beautiful and there are so many kinds of flowers and plants in the world. One could spend years exploring and capturing all the various types. The perfect photography garden will consist of plants that bloom all year round, but, thanks to full fledged winters, I personally don't have such a garden. However, I do have some flowers that my wife has graciously planted, and my hometown has parks and such where there are opportunities aplenty for this type of work.

With a flower that has a distinct stamen, the part that contains the pollen, I often find myself drawn to keep that in focus. It's like photographing people or animals and making the eyes the part that needs to

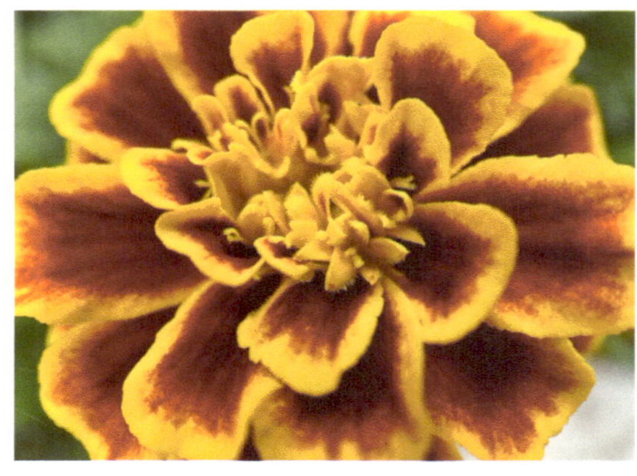

A flower in a public park.

be sharp. With such a shallow depth of field to work with, getting the stamen sharp will most likely result in the petals being blurred, which is fine, but adjusting your angle can be advantageous in getting them both in focus. I will look for the edge of a petal to be

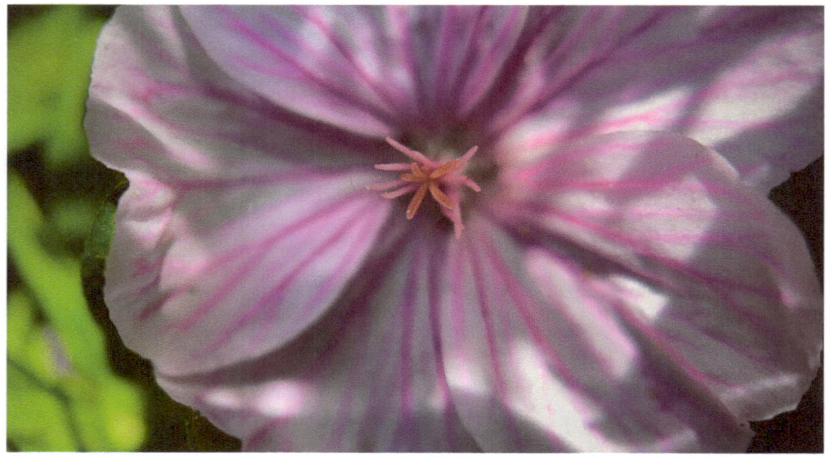

The petal's edge and stamen are in focus.

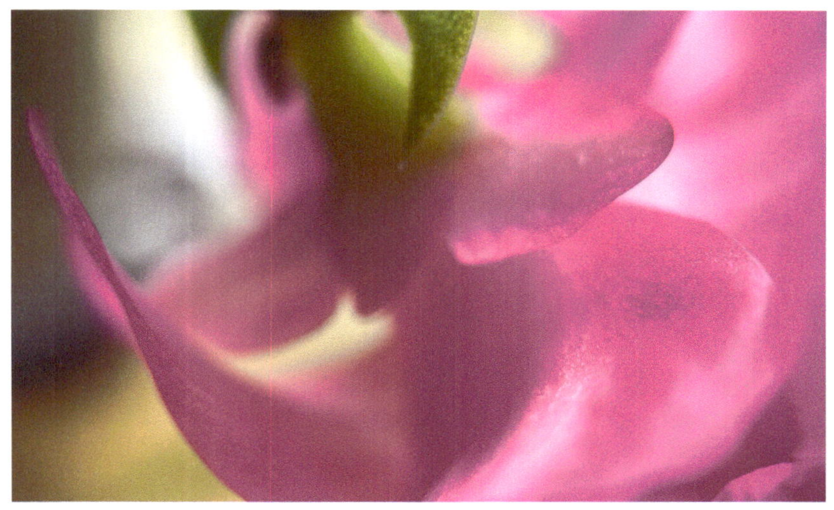

African Violet with the petal edges in focus.

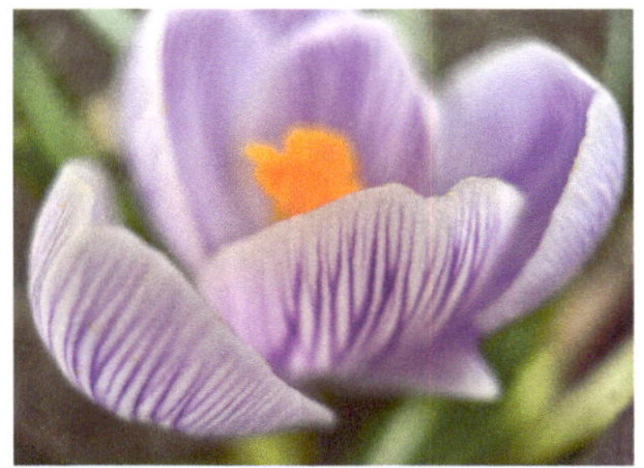

Focused on the petal.

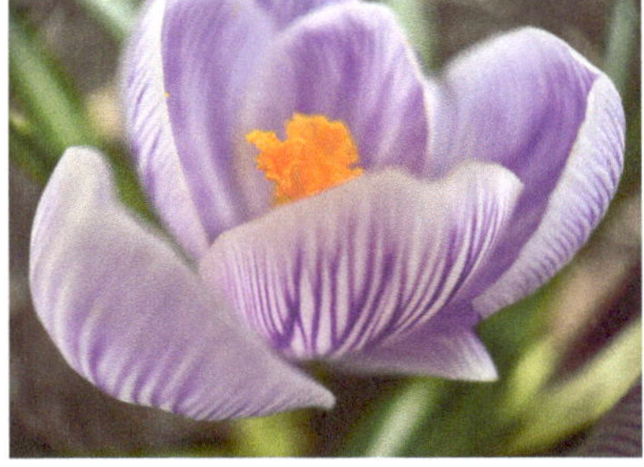

Focused on the stamen.

crisp while tilting the iPhone ever-so slightly to also get a sharp view of the stamen.

Petals come in so many shapes and sizes so, there's never a right or wrong way to capture them. Getting the edge of a petal sharp will always give you a good result, but sometimes featuring a blemish or water droplet in the middle of a petal can be just as aesthetically pleasing. Shooting at such an angle where you have an edge of a petal in sharp focus while the rest of the frame is filled with blurred shades and tones can make for amazing abstract images. A complete series of prints used for wall decor can be found on a single bloom but be mindful of your white balance here because if you don't lock it in place, you'll have issues with colour consistency. Something to try is to capture a flower with the edge of a petal in focus, then take another shot while ignoring the petals and focusing on the stamen to see how the two images differ.

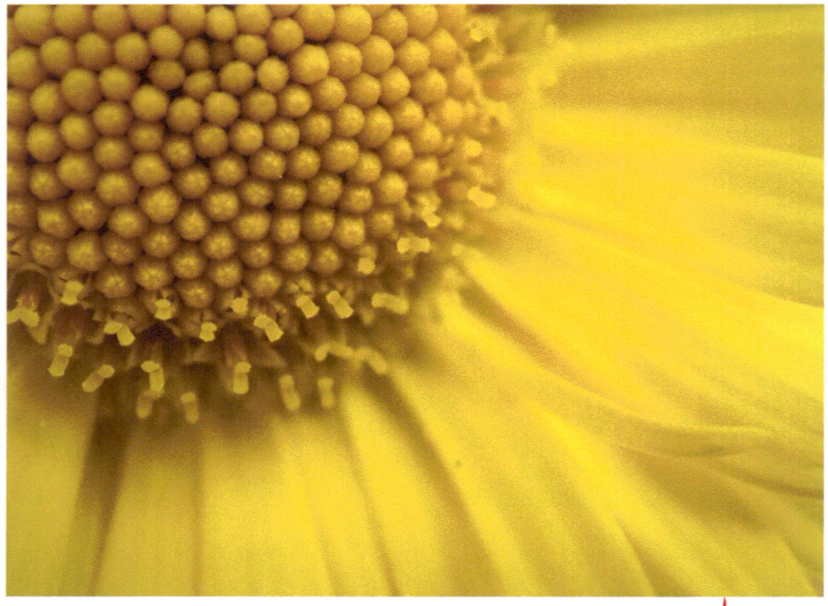

How would this look as a large print?

Small daisies are some of my favourite flowers to shoot because when they are shot in macro, they obviously look bigger, but they also allow you to get more of the complete flower in the frame. This offers some interesting compositions. This yellow daisy was shot with the macro lens over the Telephoto camera on an iPhone 8 Plus and it's one of my favourite daisy images. An acquaintance once told me it would look nice as a very big enlargement, so one day I'll take his advice and get it done.

Dandelions in their seeding state are wonderful to photograph, either in their natural habitat or plucked and brought indoors. While

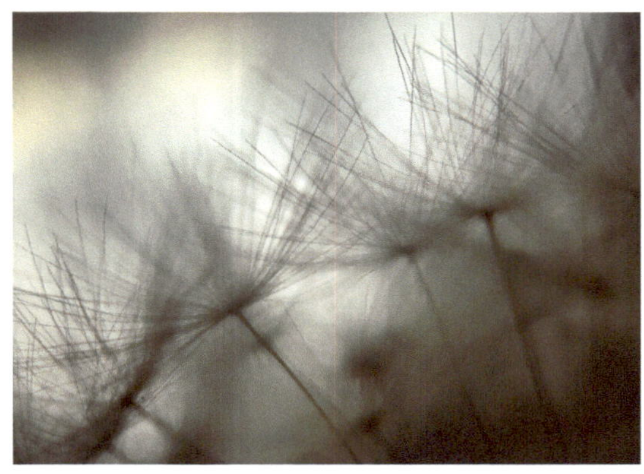

Dandelion seeds focused on the tips.

walking our dog, I spotted a perfectly round, completely full seed-head, so I picked it, being careful not to lose any of the seeds. I brought it home and put together a makeshift stand and clip to prop it into position. You could get creative here with lighting and backgrounds for different artistic impressions. When I shot the seed-head, I used natural light from a nearby window and the wall behind was burgundy, which turned out to be too dark. As an experiment, I dug out a box of old photographs and placed photos with lightly coloured shades behind as a

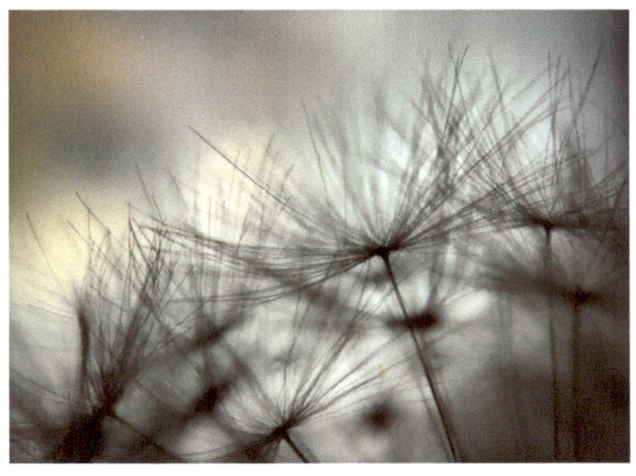

Dandelion seeds focused on the stems.

backdrop. It didn't matter what the image was in the photo, because it would be nothing but a blur more than an inch behind my subject. The selected photos offered a bright enough backdrop that I was able to continue shooting in natural light.

On this particular occasion, I put the lens over the Telephoto camera to get in nice and close while focusing on different parts of the seeds. When focus is set on the stem of a seed, the little hairs, called pappus, at the end of the stem are like ribs on an umbrella that lost its canopy. They would intersect with the pappus of the other seeds creating what looked like a bunch of sticks that exploded at the ends. Shift the focus away from the stem and the pappus would be sharp in other areas while the blurred stems offered a much softer, dreamy composition. I recommend having the iPhone on a tripod when shooting something like this, but more on that later.

PLANTS

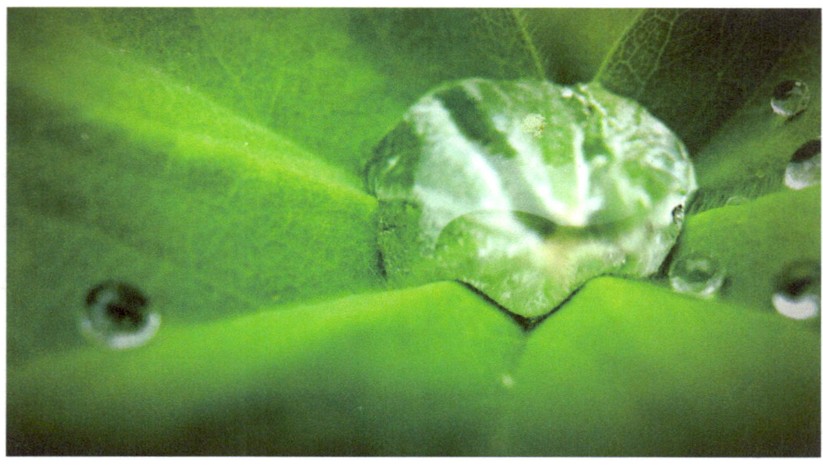

A large water droplet in the centre of a Lupin's leaf.

Aside from flowers, other plant life can offer a vast amount of possibilities for macro capture. I love the colour green when doing photography, like the greens of a forest or meadow during summer. What makes shooting green plants extra fun for me is when there are water droplets on the leaves. Depending on the species, the water could be sitting in the centre of the plant which can give the droplet a unique shape. We once had lupins in our flower bed and before the flowers would bloom, the leaves offered deep valleys leading to the centre where droplets would be in abundance after a rain. Of course, you don't always have to rely on a rainfall to have droplets. A quick spray with a garden hose or watering can will leave droplets wherever you need them, and on a clear day, the sun will make the water sparkle and the greens will look bright and saturated.

Glycerin mixed with water and a hypodermic needle can also be a handy set of tools in your macro arsenal. Water alone tends to lose its grip on whatever it may be clinging to, especially if there is a breeze. With the needle, you can strategically place glycerin drops on various places throughout a plant, and with the right lighting and a good background, a macro lens will pick up some wonderful, inverted reflections of that background creating images within the image.

I live in a city that surrounds a portion of the Niagara Escarpment so trails

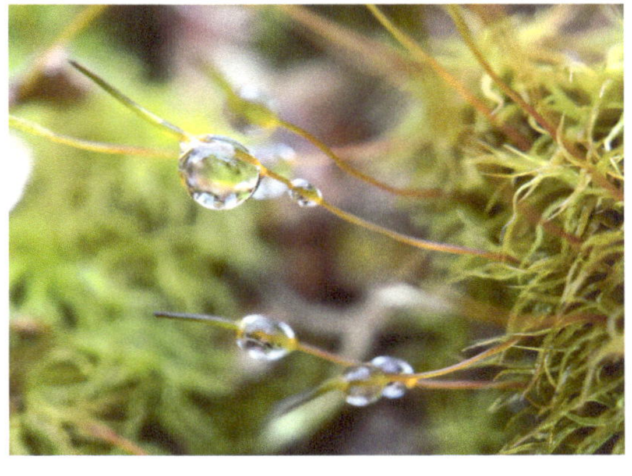

Droplets on moss like marshmallows on a stick.

and wooded areas are all around me. I'll always take my macro lens with me when exploring these areas because you never know what you'll see. The forest floor is host to a variety of ferns, fungus and

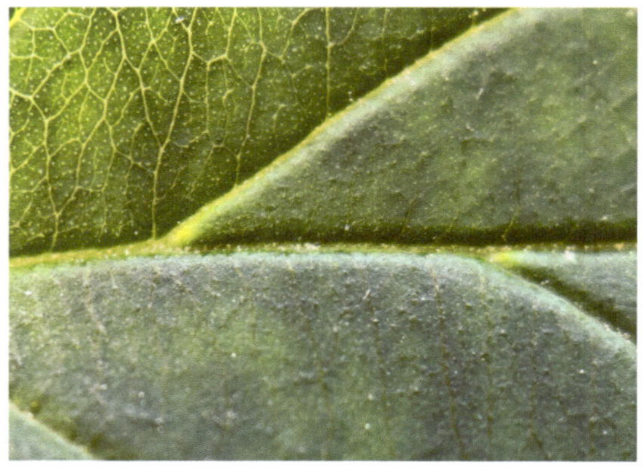

The texture of a leaf.

moss. After a rain, stop where moss grows on rocks or trees and get down close. The leafy shoots of the moss will hold small droplets of water like a stick holding a marshmallow. Now that's a strange analogy, isn't it? Be creative with your angle of approach here too, because getting low and aiming the phone up where you get better light from the sky can add some welcomed refraction to the droplet.

Plants and trees offer quite a variety of textures and patterns that are easily emphasized with macro. A simple leaf from any tree, when viewed through a macro lens, will reveal the intricate system of veins that

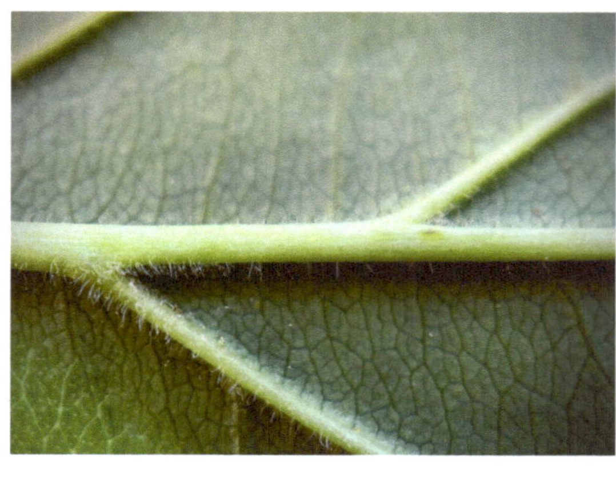

The veins on the underside of a leaf.

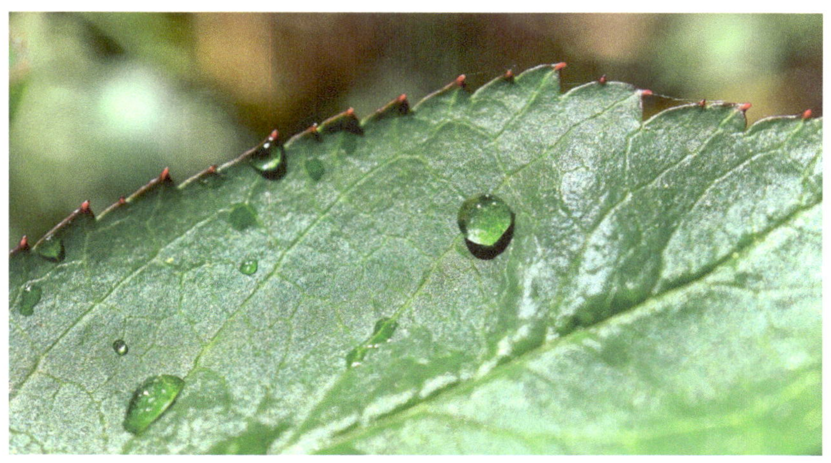

The edge of a leaf is called the margin.

give the leaf structure and carry water throughout the blade. The
larger veins also transport chlorophyll created by the leaf back to the
stem and into the plant. Most leaves are curved making it tricky to
get much of the structure in focus. Try shooting it with the midrib,
the large vein that runs down the centre and connects to the stem, on
an even plane with the lens to make it the main subject. The way the
blade on either side fades to blurred oblivion can be somewhat
surreal, and shooting the underside of a leaf could give you more
detail and texture.

The edge of a leaf known as the margin, can offer the same
interest in images as the edge of a petal on a flower. We had a shrub
that would flower in late spring and the pollen that fell from the
blossoms would gather on the leaves below. On one particular day,
the edges of the leaves were curled up and the pollen was stuck to
the little points along the margin. I'd never seen anything like it. As I
explored the shrub, I found places where the blossoms had detached

themselves and fallen onto the leaves, which made for some interesting photos.

Be sure to take a closer look at the various plants around you, from the smallest weed to the biggest tree, where the texture of the bark can draw you in to capture dozens of photos. Some plants, like the TriColoured Willow shrub, have very interesting leaves, and I never realized how different they were until I got a closer look at the one in our back yard.

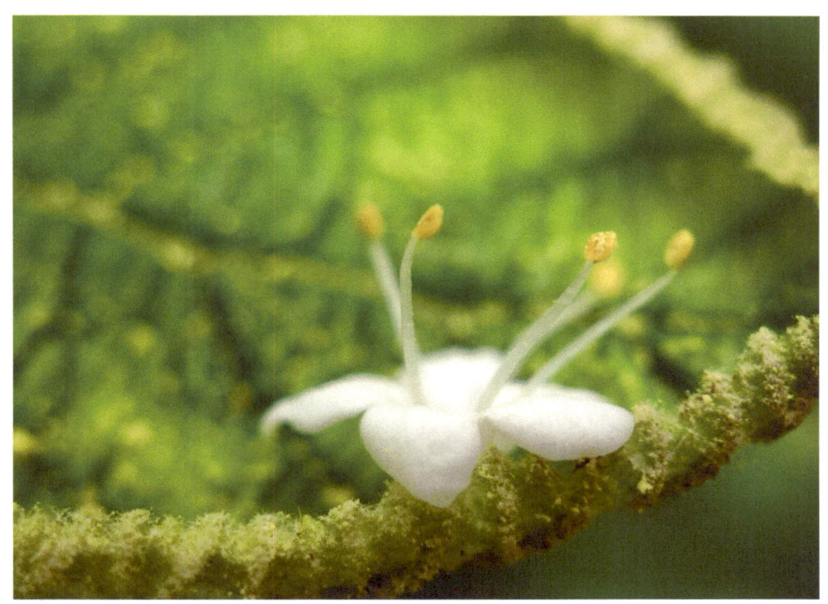

A leaf coated with pollen with a fallen blossom.

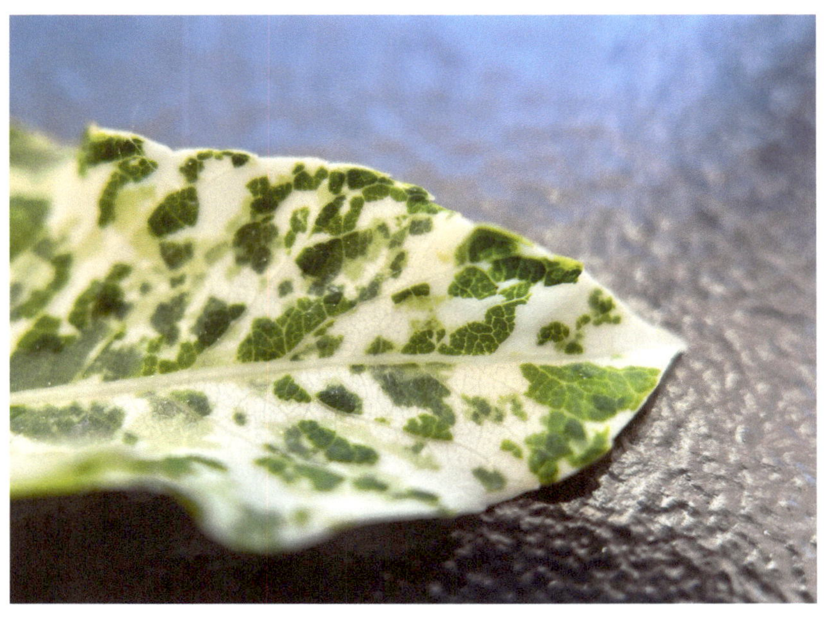

A tricoloured dappled Willow leaf.

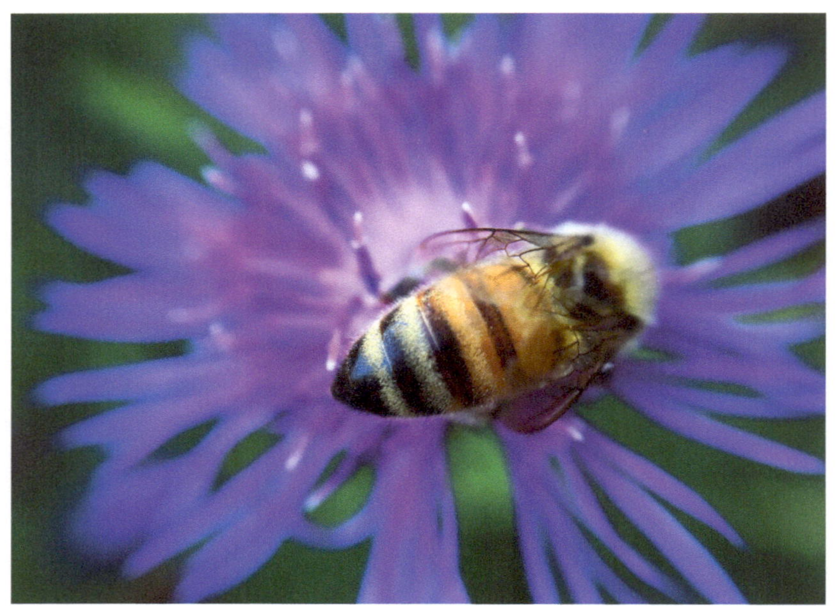

Chapter 5 - Insects

As you can well imagine, insects make amazing macro subjects and I love to photograph them. Some insects give me the willies, though, like tent caterpillars but that's only when I run into them unexpectedly. When I can approach them on my terms, they don't bother me, and I can get in close for a shot or two. Viewing insects through a macro lens will show details about them that we simply wouldn't have known to exist. One thing I should note here is that if you don't know what kind of insect it is, be cautious with it because it could be an endangered species or a type of insect with a lethal defence attribute. You should be very cautious of spiders.

SPIDERS

Every year I can find spiders in my back yard, and their ability to create a web never ceases to amaze me. Capturing a macro shot of a spider in its web can be tedious because the slightest breeze can make the web wiggle and knock things out of focus. Approach the web slowly, but be mindful that you can

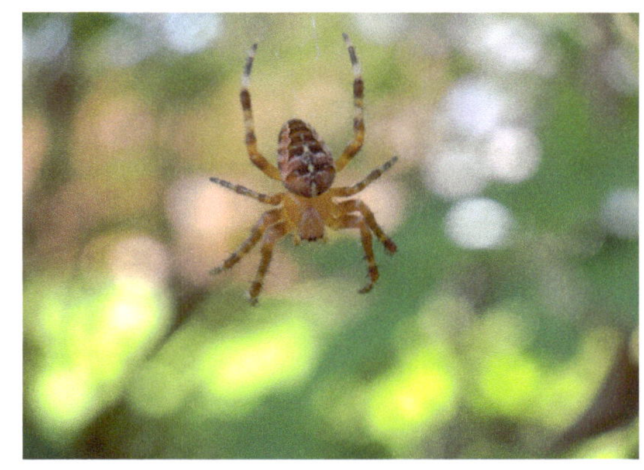

The Cross Orb Weaver Spider.

easily startle the spider and cause it to take off quickly. Another thing to be careful about is the fact that your hand can make contact with the web if you move in at the wrong angle. You need to have your iPhone parallel to the web to not only avoid disturbing the spider, but this will also give you the best angle for capturing the little fellow.

Spiders make interesting subjects from both the top and bottom side, as it allows us to get a good look at them

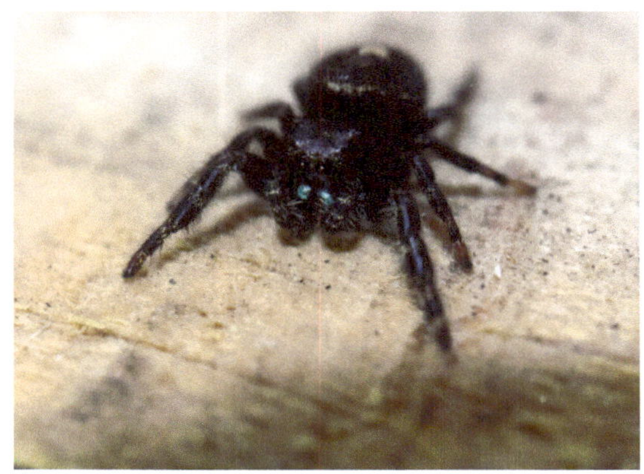

The Bold Jumping Spider.

and see the intricate details of their anatomy. When shooting from the top side, try to get their eyes in focus, just like with any other creature. It's hard to do, of course, but if you take enough photos of it, you're bound to be successful. If shooting from directly above the spider and the eyes aren't clearly in the shot, this is a good opportunity to showcase some of the markings on the body or legs. Shooting from the underside of a spider can showcase other details, like how the legs attach to the body.

The spider's web is created for many reasons and one of them is to capture and store food. This gives one the opportunity to get photos of other types of insects.

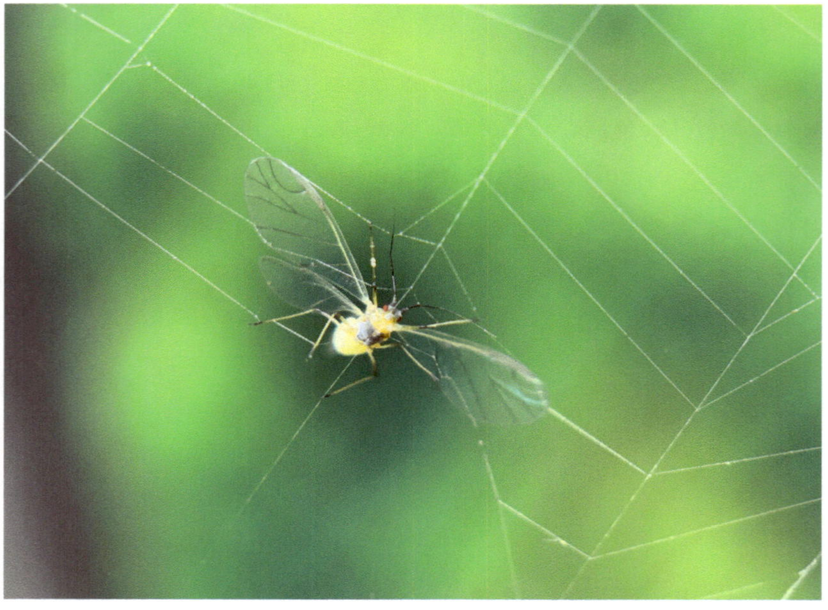

A Gnat caught in a spider's web.

ANTS

These little six-legged busy bodies are fun to watch and even more fun to photograph. They're solely responsible for wasting a few hours of my time over the years because they move fast and getting a perfect shot of one isn't easy. Be prepared to spend some time on them, especially if they're on flowers because they don't stay in one place for long. The typical Black Garden Ant is the most common type where I live and the females will try to do their part in the pollination of plants and flowers so they can be seen gathering pollen. The biggest challenge is getting the right part of the ant in focus, and since the eyes are harder to see on ants, just getting the head in sharp focus is a bonus.

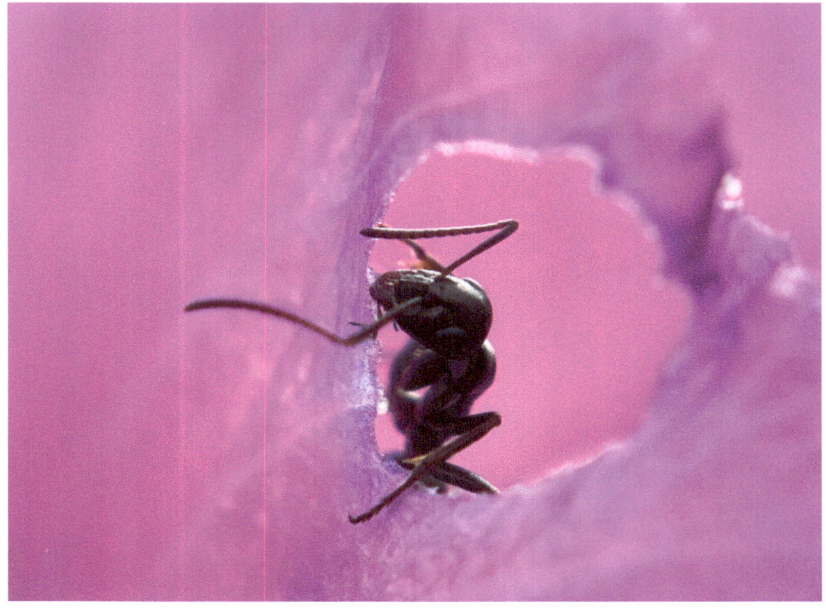

The Black Garden Ant.

One trick I know will work is to put some sugar water on a surface, outdoors of course, where it can attract some ants. If you've ever put up a hummingbird feeder I'm sure you've seen ants crawling all over it. Let the ants gather around the sugar water then, trying not to disturb them, shoot to your heart's content.

BEES

Bees are about as busy as ants when they're gathering nectar and pollen. Generally, I'd be afraid of getting stung if I got too close to a bee's business, but when they're diving into a flower, they seem to be more in tune with the task at hand and not worried so much about being photographed. Still, be careful when chasing bees around a flower bed or shrub. I'm sure they have a tolerance threshold when

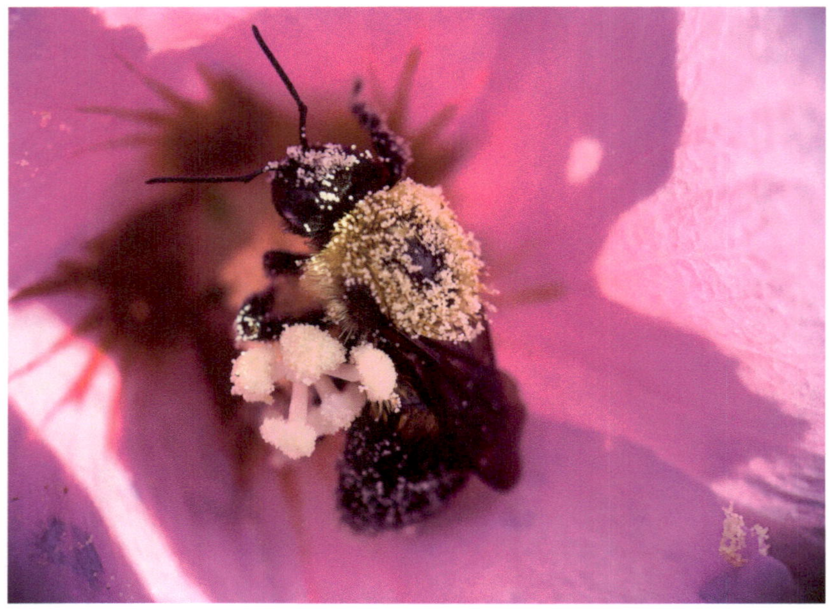

A bee covered in pollen.

you're holding an iPhone just centimetres away from them while they're working.

As with flowers, I can't identify the different types of bees or wasps without the internet, but I treat them all with the same amount of respect. The best image I've taken of a wasp was the result of it having a lot of patience with me as I spent about two minutes taking as many shots as I needed to get the eyes sharp and properly focused.

I can't stress enough how important it is to be careful around bees, or any insect for that matter. If you think they are getting the least bit agitated by your presence, move on to another spot. You may get lucky, like I did with the docile wasp, but don't take it for granted that they will never sting you.

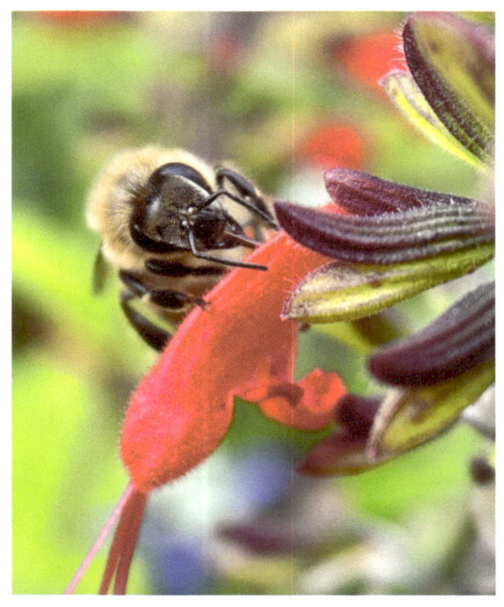

Captured with the Struman Optics Cinematic Macro lens.

BUGS IN GENERAL

There are thousands, if not millions of insect species in the world and our planet couldn't exist as we know it without them. So exploring their tiny part of the globe is something I consider to be a privilege. I could research and write a section about many different kinds of bugs, but I think the best advice I could give here is to take some time out of your day, when you can, and see what they're all about. If your iPhone has both a Main and Telephoto camera, try a macro lens over each of them to get the best look possible at your subject. Sometimes the difference you see in the details is well worth the effort.

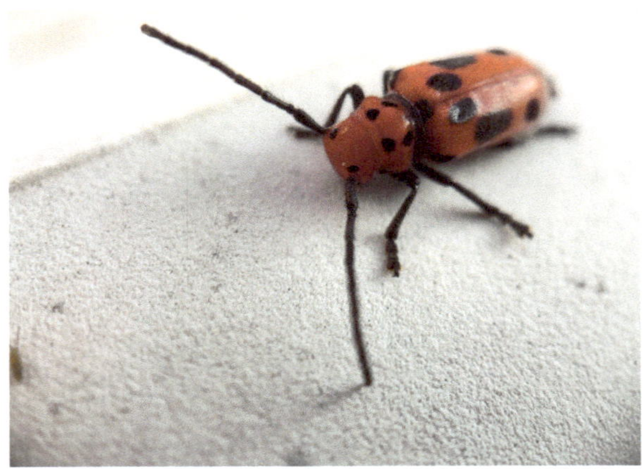

A Red Milkweed Beetle shot with a Moment Macro lens
on the 1x camera of a XS Max.

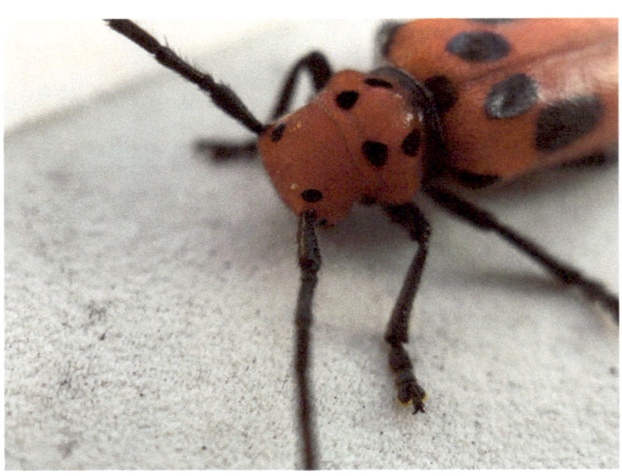

This time the beetle was with the Moment Macro on the
2x camera of the XS Max.

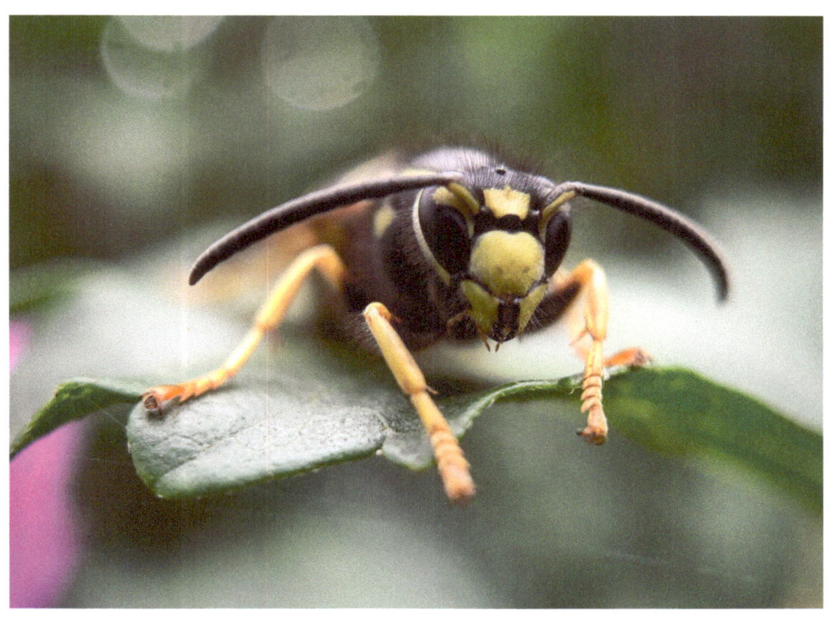

One of the best macro photos I've taken.

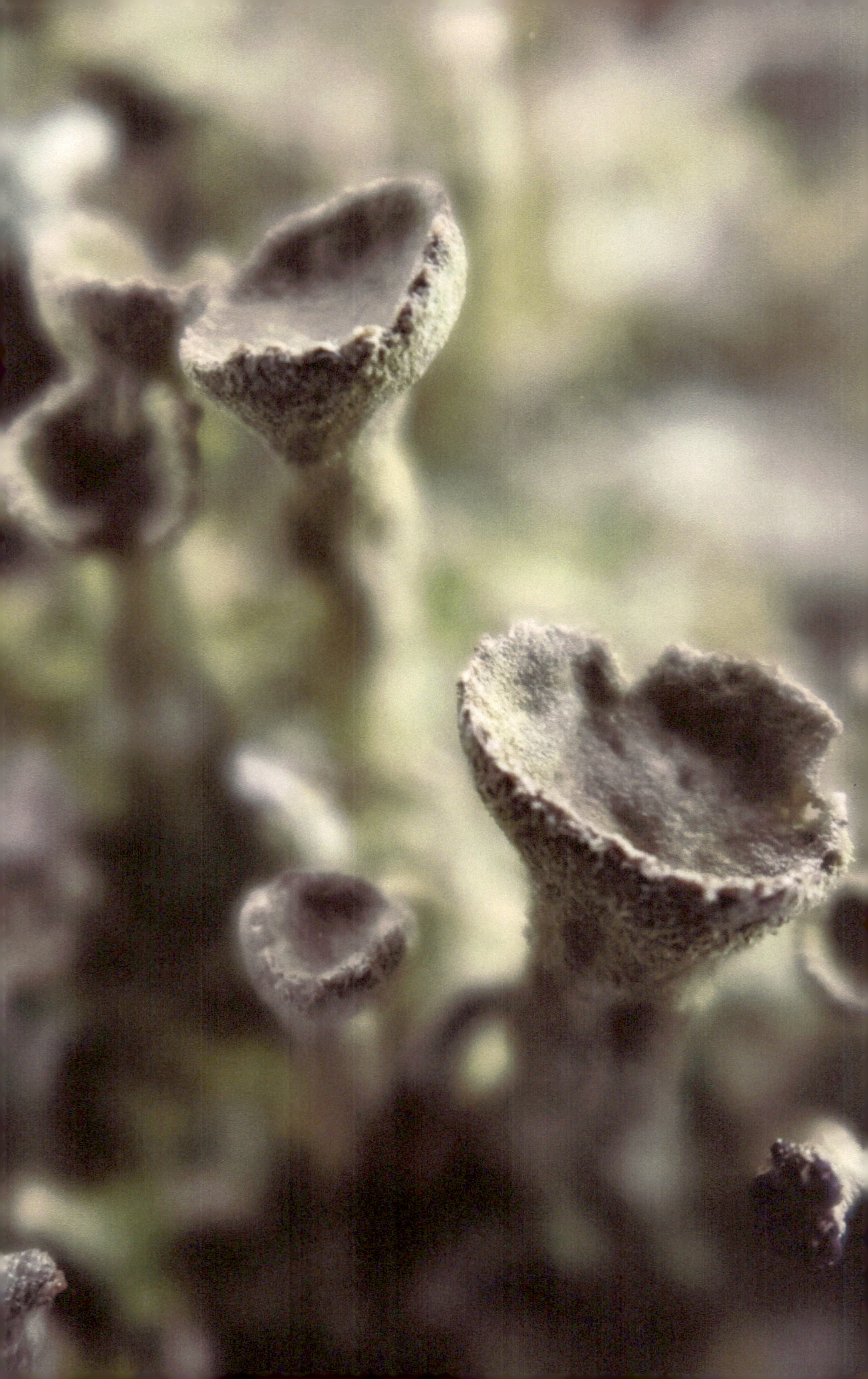

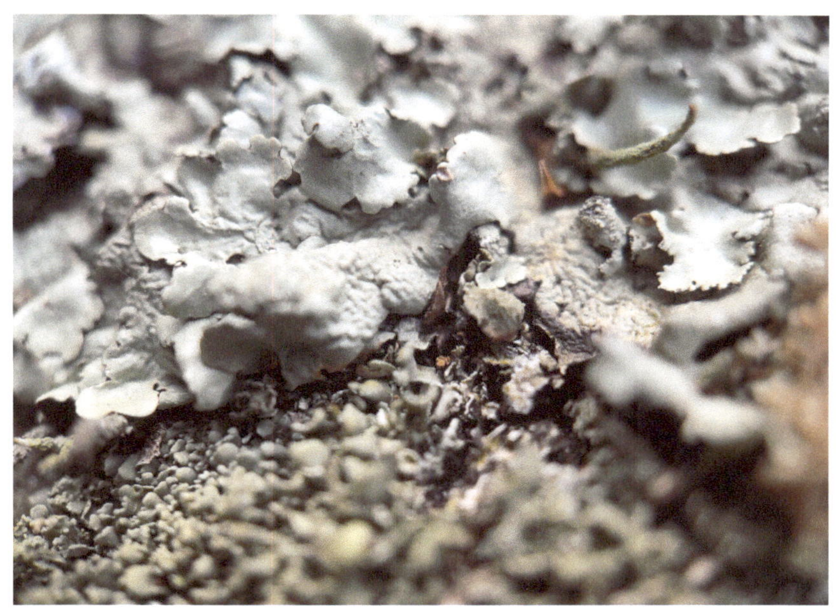

Chapter 6 - Research

The purpose of doing research is to gain more knowledge of a given topic or subject, or to learn something new altogether. There are a number of steps in the research process including: realizing the problem you're trying to solve, figuring out what you already know, developing your research process, collecting your data, documenting your findings, and coming up with the results. Part of the data collection process could very well include taking photos.

The iPhone comes with a Magnifier built into the operating system. This is an accessibility feature that uses the camera as a magnifying glass to help you see things up close, like small type, but it doesn't get as close as you may want if you're trying to do a little research on something. This is where a macro lens will work much better.

LICHEN

Earlier, I talked about shooting moss on rocks and trees, but there's another form of growth worth exploring which could easily fit into Chapter 4, but it serves as a great research topic. Lichen is a composite organism that arises from algae living amongst fungi and can be found in so many different places, the most common in my experience being headstones in a cemetery, on old wooden fences, and on trees. An image search for lichen revealed to me that it exists in numerous forms.

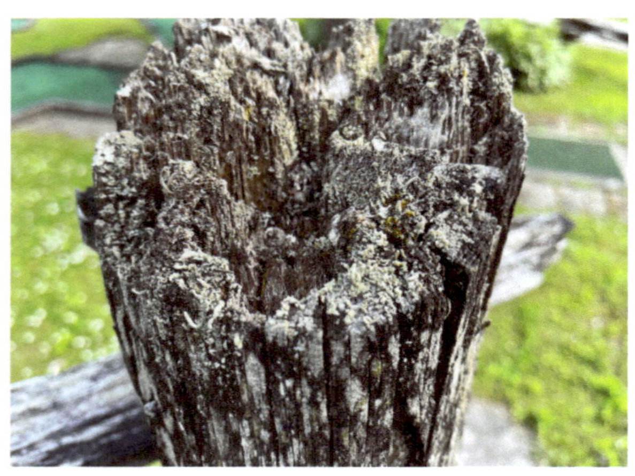

Lichen on a fence post.

Something I've never seen before in lichen is the "golf tee" shaped chutes growing amongst it. I found them on a fence post and wouldn't have noticed them had I not started taking some photos for this book. These little hollow stalks are called podetia and can be pointed, cupped or like a club. The mere fact that I included this information in the book is a case in point that macro photography can be an important part of doing research because if I'm being honest, I really didn't know that much about lichen.

RESEARCH IN GENERAL

Research can be as complicated or simple as you like. One could spend years exploring a problem and perhaps never find the answer, but when the problem isn't so complex, getting to that "ah ha" moment can come sooner than later and be very rewarding. Using macro photography is just one of the many data collection tools available when conducting research. Imagine what we could find out about insects while researching with a macro lens.

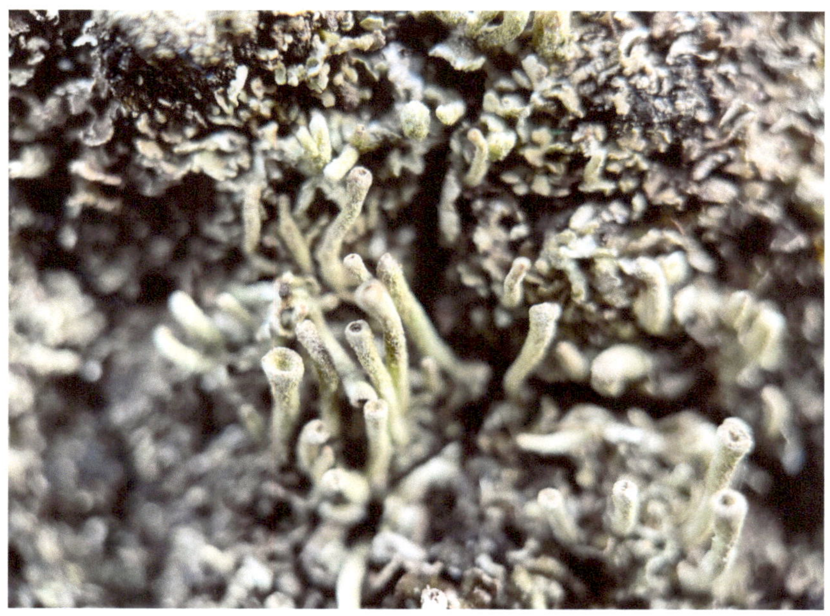

Lichen Podetia.

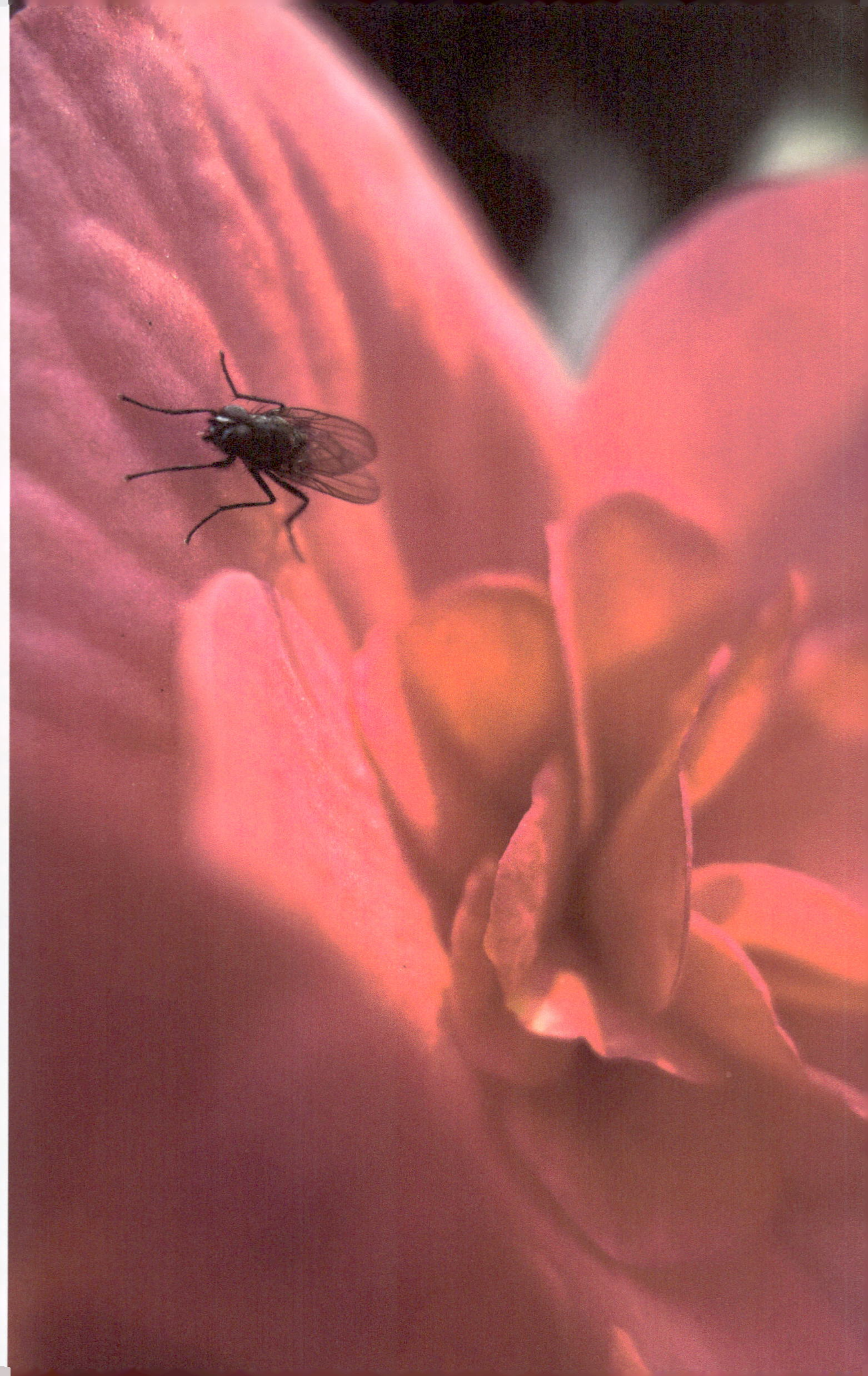

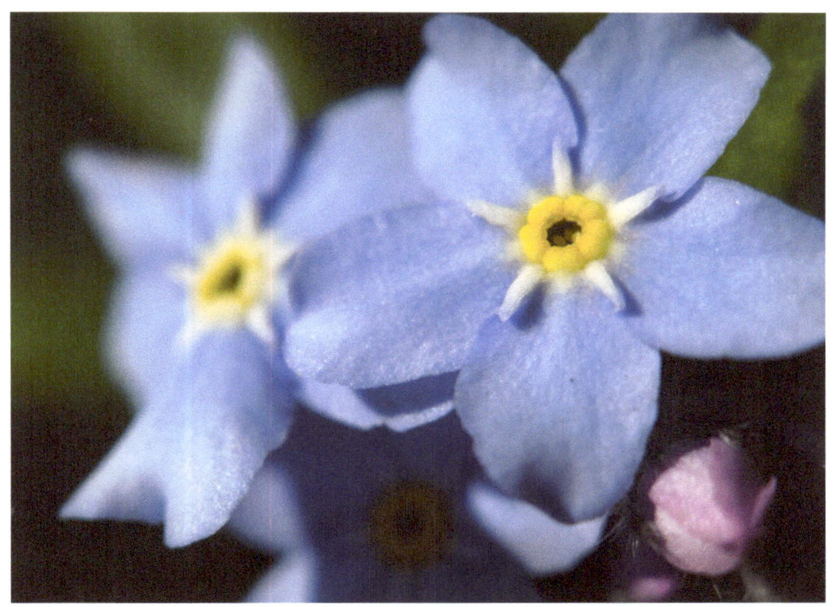

Chapter 7 - Shooting Techniques

Before you can start shooting macro properly with your iPhone, you should look at some apps that will be effective in helping you get your shots. In Chapter 1, I covered the technology behind the multi camera iPhones and why the Apple Camera app isn't always the best choice for shooting macro. While the built in camera is a viable option, I do find it to be limited in its abilities compared to some third-party apps. This chapter will show you various techniques to employ in your macro shooting, but I will also be exploring the science behind each of the topics (not in too much depth) to explain how they work so you can understand why you'll do what you do.

FOCUSING

In normal use, iPhone cameras will intelligently focus on the subject you intend to capture. They have a range of focus that will be from millimetres away from the lens to infinity. That covers a lot of area. Put a macro lens over the camera and that range of focus shrinks to mere millimetres to centimetres, so as you can imagine, there isn't much room for error when trying to focus on something.

Enter the concept of manual focusing. This technique is achieved in the Apple Camera by simply tapping on the screen to select where you want to focus. This achieves focus and also sets the exposure. What the Apple Camera app doesn't do for you is confirm exactly what is in focus. This is why focus peaking is a real asset for macro work. With so little room for error, focus peaking gets the edge of a flower's petal in sharp

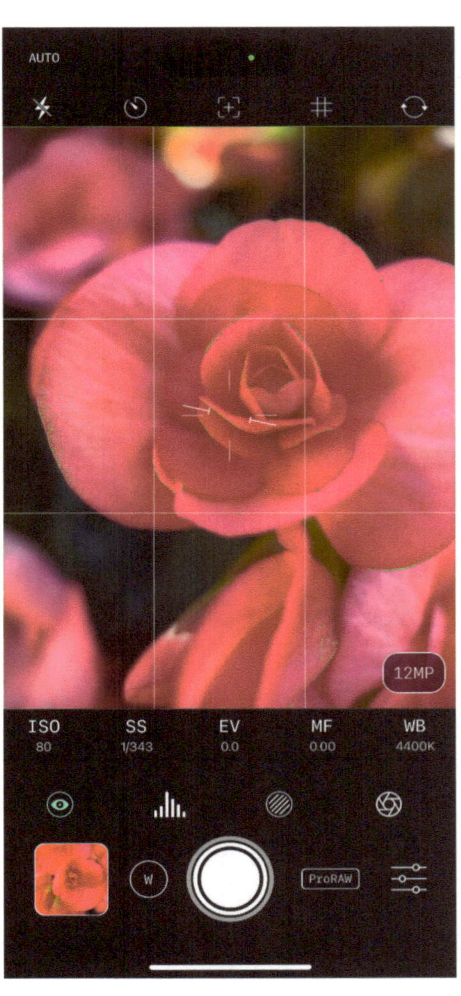

Focus Peaking in Reeflex and how it highlights the edges of the petals.

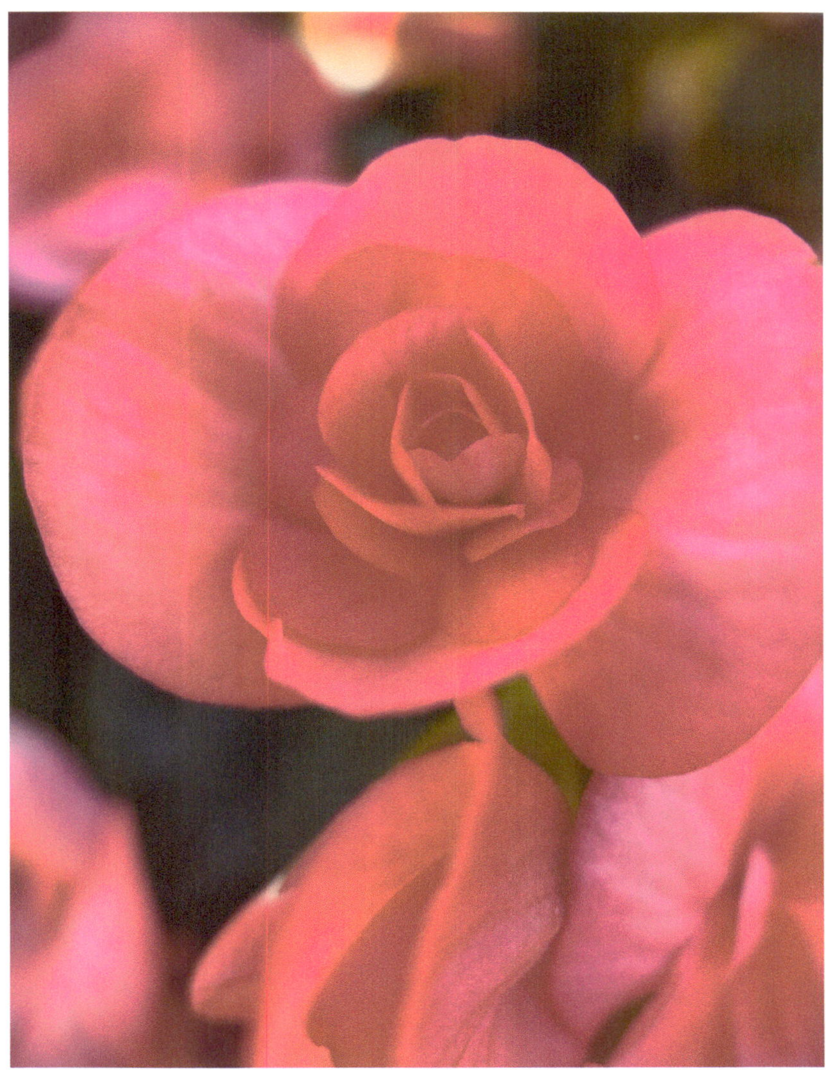

The result of Focus Peaking is sharpness where the green highlights were located.

focus relatively easy, and you don't need to waste time taking multiple frames to get one right.

The focus ring on the Struman Optics lens works like those of traditional camera lenses in that you turn the ring to achieve focus on

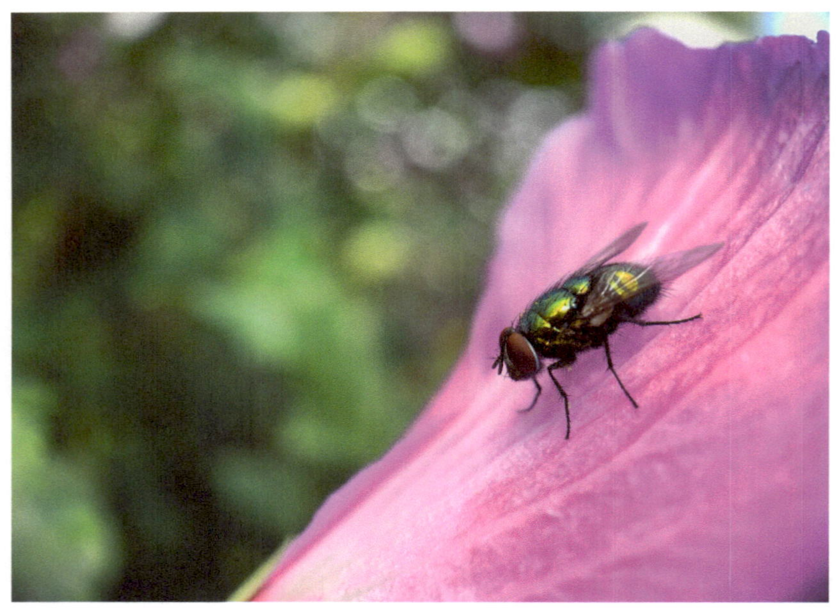

I find Focus Peaking to be one of the best assets in my macro toolkit. In these photos of a fly I was able to get he eyes sharp each time in short order.

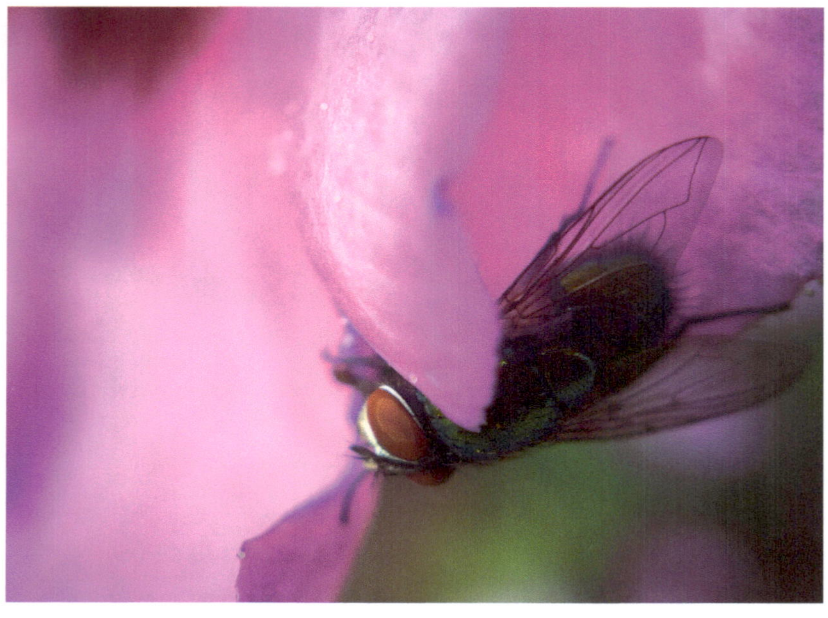

your subject. This versatility works well in autofocus since you can let the Struman lens determine how close you get to the subject. This is perfect for those times when your subject is too big for the frame because now you can get it all in the shot simply by moving back and adjusting the focus ring to compensate for the difference in distance. Alternatively, you can go full manual with your focusing but in addition to focusing with the manual controls of the camera app, you can simply turn the focus ring on the lens, and with focus peaking activated, you can get that sharp focus quickly.

MANUALLY SELECTING THE CAMERA

I touched on the technology behind Apple's multi-camera iPhones in Chapter 1 so I won't go over that again, but I will talk about why you might want to manually select the different cameras if you have them.

With a multi-camera pro model iPhone you have options when it comes to doing macro. Attachment lenses can't be used on the Ultra Wide so you have a choice between the Main camera and, if equipped, the Telephoto.

When you have a Long Range macro lens (sometimes referred to as a 75mm) over the Main camera, you will get the best image quality that the iPhone's camera can give you for a couple of reasons. The first being that the Main camera has the largest aperture which will let the most light into the sensor, thus making it possible to use a lower ISO, and that lends itself to less noise in the image.

The second reason, and likely the best reason if you have a pro iPhone starting with the 14 - or even the iPhone 15 non-pro as I write this part of the book - is that you have a 48MP sensor and can get some amazing detail in your images. But… that's not all.

With the 15 Pro Max, the Main camera has additional "focal lengths" built in when using the Apple Camera app. There's the native 1x setting, which is 24mm, but when you tap the "1x" in the camera selector, it toggles through to 1.2x (28mm) and 1.5x (35mm), plus you still have the 2x (48mm) setting. These additional focal lengths are just the result of the camera utilizing the 48MP sensor and cropping down to give you a smaller than full resolution file with each option.

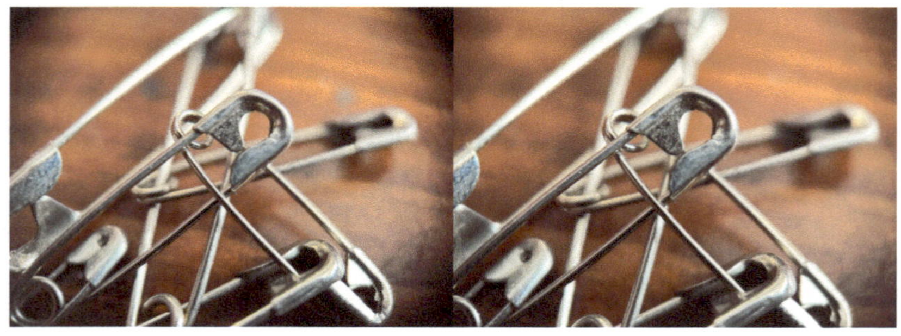

Long Range Macro lens on Main Camera using Apple Camera app.
24mm and 28mm focal lengths.

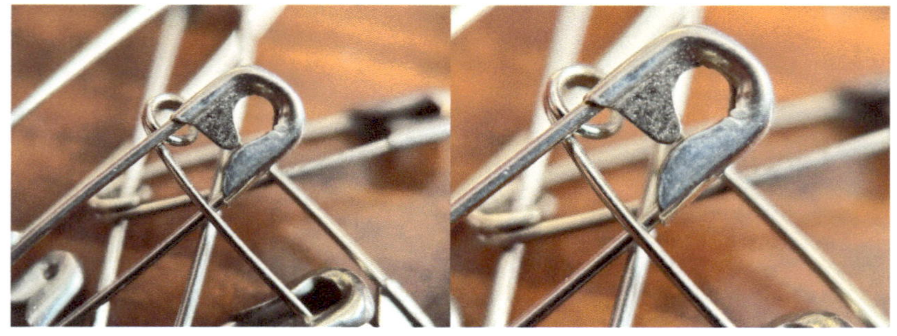

Long Range Macro lens on Main Camera using Apple Camera app
35mm and 48mm focal lengths.

The Apple Camera app can be confusing at times because it is more versatile than most people realize, and here's why I'm saying this: with the 48MP Pro model camera, those additional focal lengths will all give you a 24MP file unless you do one thing, and that is to enable the camera to shoot in its maximum resolution. To do that, go to Settings > Camera > Formats, make sure ProRAW and Resolution Control is toggled on, then underneath that, go to Pro Default. Here you select either HEIF Max (or JPG Max, depending on the file type you use) or ProRAW Max. When this is all turned on, you can long press the format indicator in the top right of the camera's viewfinder and select the Max option, whether it's JPG, HEIF, or RAW (which is ProRAW).

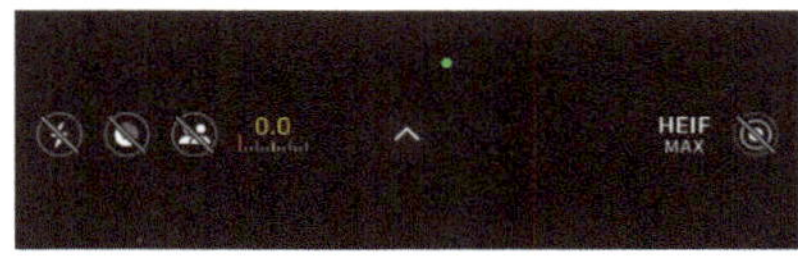

Apple Camera File Select
that reads "HEIF Max".

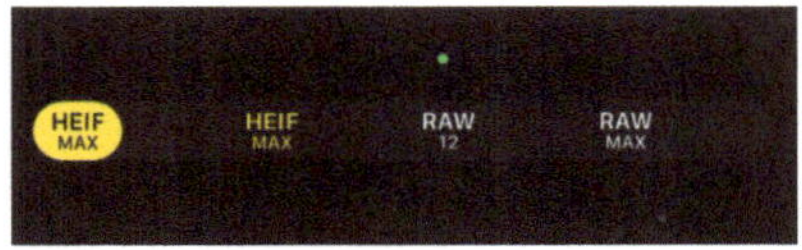

File Select option open. HEIF Max
selected and is highlighted in yellow.

Once you have your Apple Camera app set to shoot at its highest resolution, these focal lengths can now give you the following image sizes:

iPhone 15 Pro Max Camera App Set to Maximum Resolution

Camera Selection	Focal Length	File Resolution	Pixel Dimensions
1x	24mm	48MP	8064 x 6048
1.2x	28mm	35MP	6912 x 5148
1.5x	35mm	*24MP	5172 x 4284
2x	48mm	12MP	4032 x 3024
		* This is actually 22 MP but the phone's EXIF says 24MP	

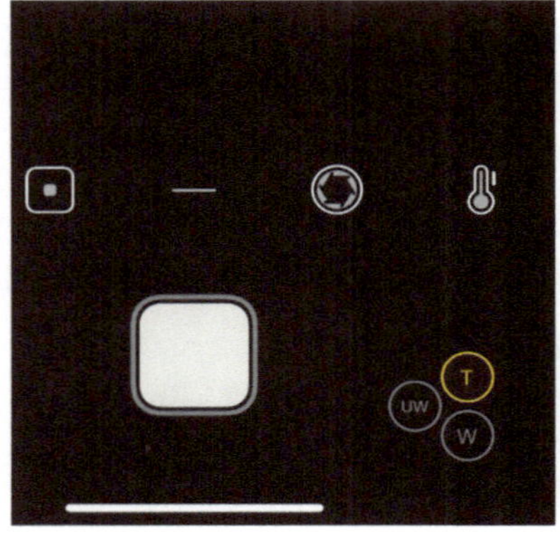

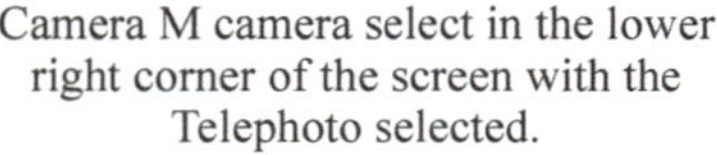

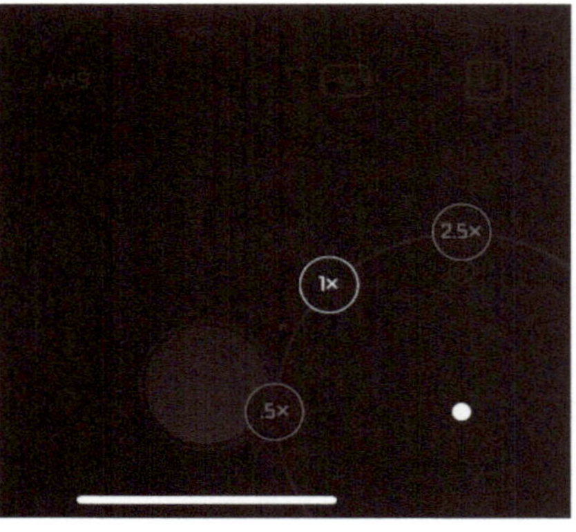

Camera M camera select in the lower right corner of the screen with the Telephoto selected.

Halide camera select also in the lower right corner but with the Main camera selected.

If the Apple Camera app is so versatile, you may be asking why you would want to use a third party app. Quite simply, if you want to get in closer to your subject than the Main camera will allow, you might decide to put your macro lens over the Telephoto camera. Since the Apple Camera doesn't always use the Telephoto when it's selected, the only option is to use a third party app because they WILL use the Telephoto. The caveat here is that the image quality from the true Telephoto is never as good as the Main camera, especially with macro. Landscape is a different story.

So, why go through all this when I'm simply talking about switching cameras? Well, depending on your subject or the purpose for your final image, using one camera over the other could make a big difference in the photo. If you really need to get in close to get the best possible view of your subject, maybe the Telephoto is the camera to use. But, if you need the best image quality, you may have to sacrifice closeness for clarity. I felt it was only fair to explain how the two cameras types will perform so you don't go from one to the other thinking you will get the same results each time. My best possible advice here would be to make sure you have lots of light to play with.

BURST MODE

One of the best utilities of the Apple Camera is Burst Mode. A few camera apps have Burst Mode, including ProCamera, Camera M, Camera Pixels and Moment.

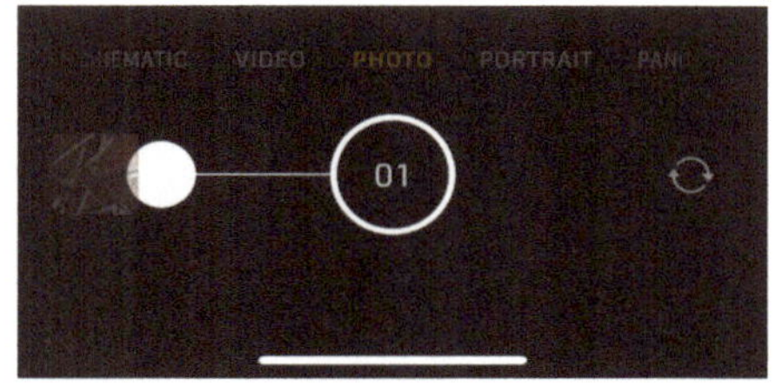

Drag your finger to the left quickly to shoot a burst of photos.

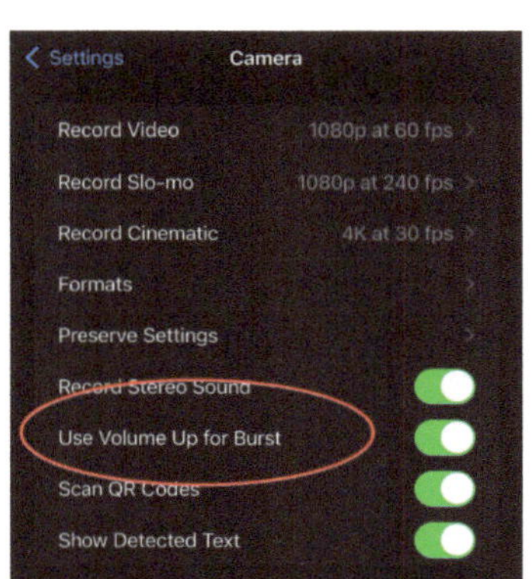

Make sure this is turned on to use the Volume Up button as a shutter.

When I want to use it, I'll use Apple's built in Camera app as long as it can do the job. If I need more control over the settings or I need to use the Telephoto, I'll choose one of the other apps. Burst Mode isn't something that needs to be selected, but you have to know how to activate it when shooting.

In 2019 when the iPhone 11 series was released, Burst Mode was changed from long pressing the shutter to tapping the shutter then dragging your finger to the Preview thumbnail in the corner of the screen. The other way to use Burst Mode is to use the Volume Up button, but that has to be enabled in the Settings app under Camera.

So, what exactly is Burst Mode and why would you use it? Burst Mode is shooting exposures at a rate of 10 frames per second. That's fast. The frames will go as long as you're shooting the sequence but, if my quick search on the internet is accurate, there's a limit of 600 frames then it stops exposing. The nice thing about digital photography is that you can shoot all you want and if you don't need all those photos, you can just delete them. In macro photography, Burst Mode would be an excellent way to ensure you get what you want as sharp as you can thanks to the very fast shutter speed it employs. Let's refer back to shooting ants. They're quick, and they don't care if you get the shot or not before they move around. Shooting 10 frames per second should increase your odds of getting something usable. Flowers are light so they move around in the breeze. Burst Mode is your friend here too. If you're like me, you want the stamen to be the point of focus in a flower shot so if you take a series of 20 or 30 shots you're bound to get one right. Another method for a successful shot is to approach the subject slowly, and when you are

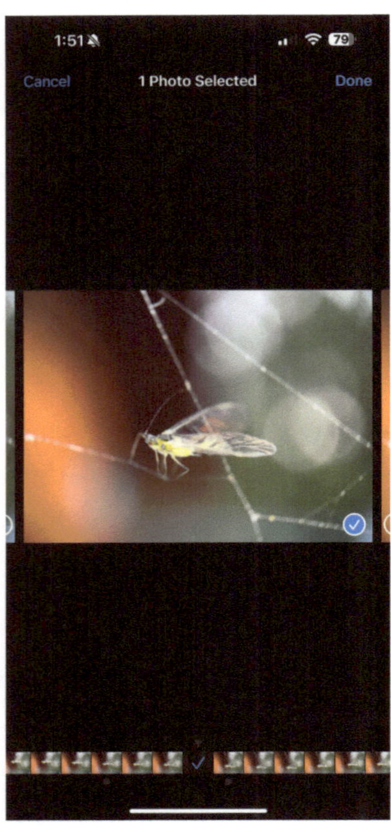

Tap "Select…" and choose a Key image as indicated by the blue check.

about to see it come into focus, start your burst and follow through until you've gone through the various focus points, then stop exposing.

When you take a series of burst images, the iPhone saves them in a cluster and uses its on-board artificial intelligence to select the sharpest frame as the "Key" image. This is the image that is displayed in the Photos app. You can manually select the Key image by selecting the burst image in your Photos Library, tapping on "Select…" at the bottom of the screen, and scrolling left or right through the series of frames. The frame that was selected by the iPhone will have a dot under it. When the frame you like is displayed, tap the circle at the lower right corner of the photo to put a check mark in it. You can select more than one frame to keep as a favourite, and this is not to be confused with images in the Favourites Album, but rather saves them as separate photos in your camera roll. To be more clear, they are just a shortcut to the original frame that was part of the burst, much

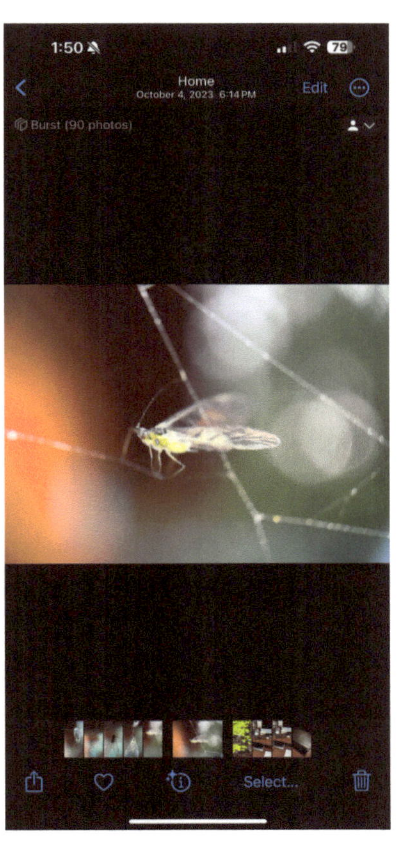

A series of burst images in the Photos app show the number of frames in the burst and has a "Select…" button.

like the photos you put into albums. They aren't copies, just shortcuts to the originals, which is designed to save space.

This seemed to be more of a lesson on what Burst Mode is than a practical discussion about how to use it in macro photography but I felt it was important to cover it in detail because I think it's a very effective technique for getting a good capture. Burst Mode can only capture JPG or HEIC images in the Apple Camera app, even if your file format is set to RAW. Burst capture in RAW is available in some third-party camera apps but you may not always perform at ten frames per second because it takes a lot of processing to capture RAW files so quickly.

It's worth noting here, too, that shooting a Live Photo is not the same as Burst Mode. The resulting image you see as a Live Photo in the camera roll will be a full resolution image of the best quality possible, but as soon as you change the Key Photo, like you can with a Burst, the new result may be full resolution, but it will be of much lesser quality.

So, we have two different, but effective ways to capture a macro photo on the iPhone that will give you the best chance at a sharp image. Focus Peaking for those times when you can get the shot in the least amount of attempts, and Burst Mode for the opportunity to choose from a number of frames to get the best shot possible.

KEEPING YOUR SUBJECT STILL

Shooting macro outside can have its challenges, and chances are, if you're shooting outdoors, you could very well be trying to get photos of flowers or insects. Keeping insects still to get a good shot is, well, almost impossible. They can get very nervous when they see

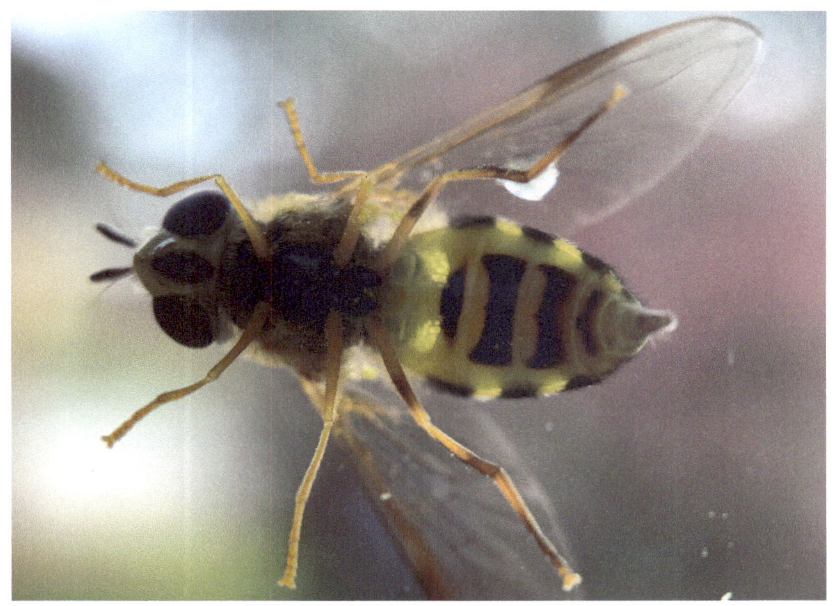

A species of fly outside my living room window.
iPhone XS Max with Moment Macro lens.

an iPhone approaching them, especially since the iPhone has to get very close to get the shot. Some insects are docile enough that they don't mind having a lens a few millimetres from their face, but I'd say, for the most part they are intimidated by something that close.

I did a little research to see what other photographers do when taking macro shots of insects and discovered that people generally sit on two different sides of a fence, with that fence being whether or not to photograph the insects in their natural habitat or use alternative methods to keep them still. I personally like to photograph them in their natural surroundings, such as in the woods, a garden, my garage, or stuck to the outside of my living room window. I'm a firm believer in capturing the world as it's presented to me.

Some folks will use a bit of science to keep insects contained within a small space to photograph them. Spreading petroleum jelly on a surface to make a circle and placing a bug in the centre will keep them there because some bugs won't walk through the jelly. I've seen examples where you can make a plexiglass box to put them in or make a little bridge out of paper clips so bugs could have somewhere to walk while you get your pictures but these types of photos just don't do it for me. I'm not saying you shouldn't resort to those methods to keep an insect still, and I don't want to start a debate on whether or not it's animal cruelty, I'm just letting you know my preference in the matter.

So, how do you keep insects still? You use your photographic skills and the capabilities of your iPhone's shutter. This is where Burst Mode will be very handy because it gives you a chance to capture your subject in sharp focus, and freeze it with a fast shutter speed. Burst Mode is one way to freeze the action, but you could also go manual with your camera app's settings.

The iPhone's camera, whether it's the Apple Camera app or a third-party app, is designed to give you the best possible shot in any given situation. When used in Auto, it will try to give you the fastest shutter speed possible while also trying to keep the ISO as low as possible. However, you have the option to have more control over the way the camera works by choosing to shoot in manual.

Most third-party camera apps will have the ability to set two of the three settings in the exposure triangle - ISO and shutter speed. The third setting of the triangle is aperture which is fixed in iPhones and can't be adjusted. A high ISO setting will allow for a faster shutter speed, but at the expense of having some digital noise in the image. When you use manual exposure in your camera app of choice and set the ISO to a higher number, the preview on the screen will get brighter. Supposing you take the ISO setting to its highest point, you will have to adjust the shutter speed to 1 over a higher number (smaller fraction) until the preview looks like it is properly exposed. You can use the histogram if the app supports it to make sure your exposure is correct.

As a totally random example, an ISO setting of 25 might require a shutter speed of 1/60th of a second for a good exposure, but if you adjust that ISO to 1000, your shutter speed may need to be adjusted to a faster speed like 1/4000th of a second. Again, totally random because the settings are completely dependant on the brightness of the scene. If your subject barely moves, use a lower ISO setting because you will get a better quality image with less noise, but if it does happen to be moving around, definitely boost the ISO for a faster shutter speed so there's no motion blur.

The same thought process goes for shutter speed too. When you adjust the shutter speed you will need to compensate with the ISO to get the exposure right, and going with a faster shutter speed will result in a higher ISO value. Also, like before, you have to keep the noise issue in mind with those faster settings.

If you're not familiar with these settings and how they work, play around with them and see how the adjustments affect your photos. There's no better way to get accustomed to your camera settings than by trying them. Also keep in mind that shooting in manual isn't always necessary, it's just an option to give you more control.

By now, you probably know there are two types of subject matter that are most common when doing macro outdoors: insects and plant life. Taller plants tend to have more movement so the slightest breeze can make a macro shot very difficult, but we were born with the most efficient tool at our disposal, our hand.

Keeping a flower still to capture that small area covered by a macro lens is as simple as holding on to it. The trick is to hold it so your hand isn't in the frame. This will likely restrict you from getting a shot from straight above so

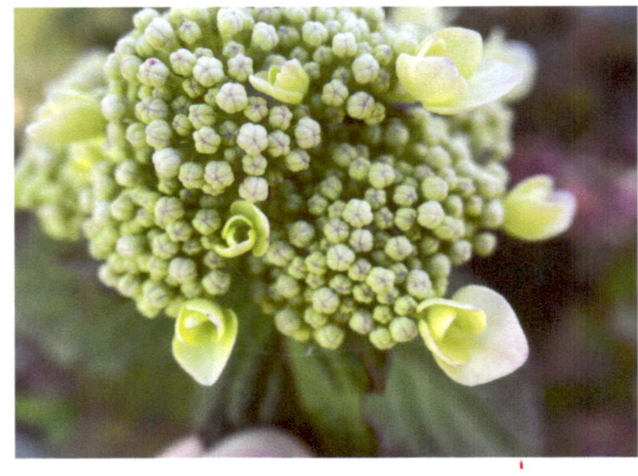

You can see my fingers at the bottom of this image as I hold the plant still in the breeze.

approach the subject from the side. If you prefer a shot from above, get close enough that you fill the frame with it so your hand won't be visible.

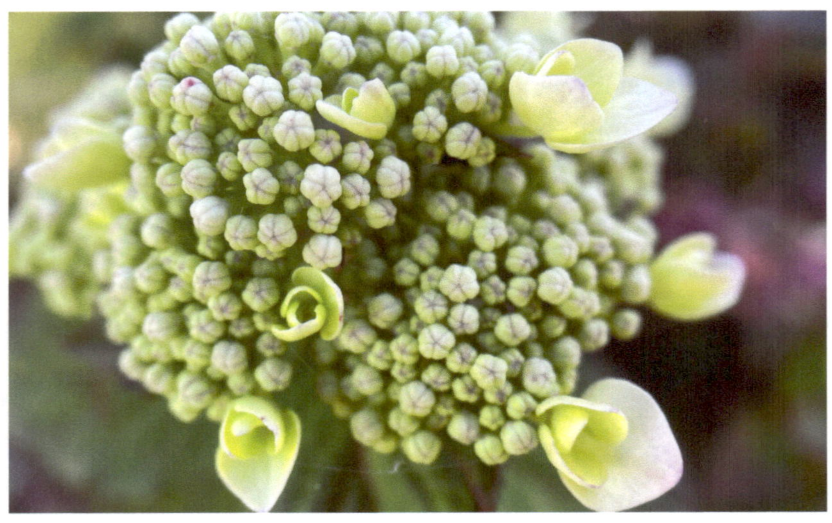

I cropped the lower part of the image to remove my fingers from the composition.

Your trusty tripod can be useful too when stabilizing a wobbly flower. You can adjust the height of the tripod so the top of it is a few centimetres below the pistil (that's the head of the flower, I looked it up) and situate the tripod so there is a leg touching one side of the stem. Set the tripod such that the flower is leaning over slightly with a little pressure on the stem to keep it from moving. This may keep the flower more stable than holding it with your hand but you will have to be mindful of the fact that the tripod legs could easily invade your composition.

DECLUTTER THE BACKGROUND

While macro photography provides for some nice bokeh, you may have situations where the background is just too busy, thus creating a rather unpleasant photo. A cluttered background could result from simply taking a shot of a flower with similar flowers behind it. You will have one in focus but the others in the background could easily draw the viewer's attention away due to the lack of interest in the photo. Look for different angles (like I haven't said that before)

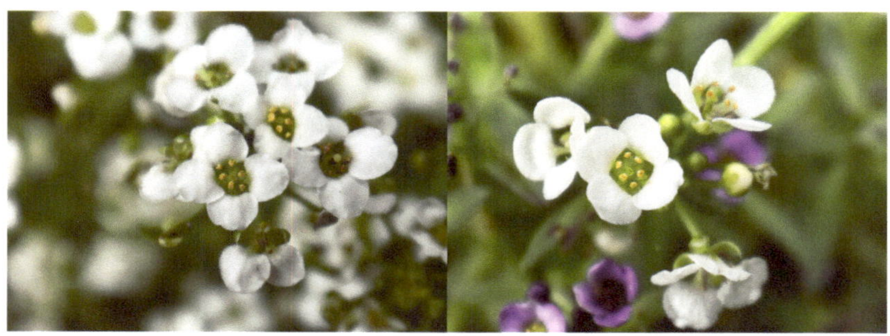

<table>
<tr><td>A cluttered background with similar subject matter.</td><td>An uncluttered background better isolates the subject.</td></tr>
</table>

where there aren't so many similar flowers in the frame. Try to isolate the flower by getting more of the green stems or leaves in the shot. Some of the stabilizing techniques will be helpful here too. For instance, you can isolate a flower from the rest by either pulling it aside, or using a tripod to hold it away from the clutter.

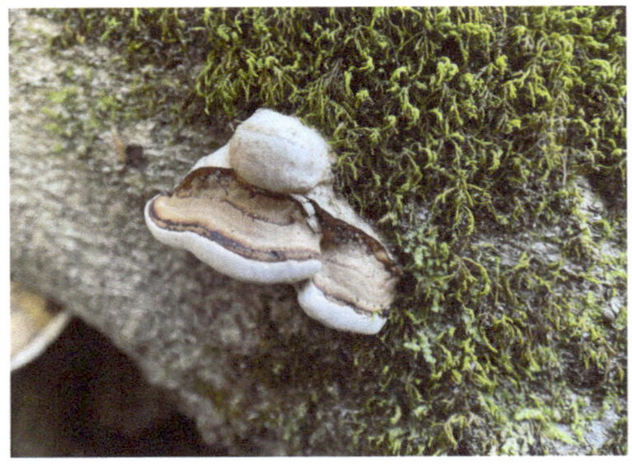

Fungi with a distracting background.

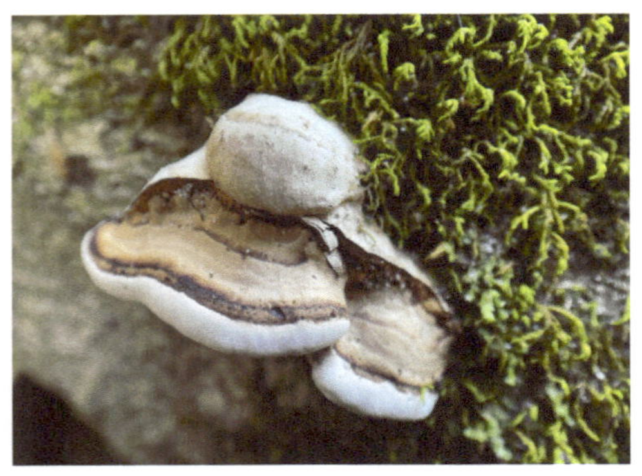

A tighter shot of the fungi brings it to the centre of attention.

If you have an iPhone with a Telephoto camera, you can put the macro lens over the Tele to better isolate your subject, even if the background contains similar features. With the Struman lens you can utilize its focus ring to get closer to your subject if you find the background doesn't fit with your vision for the shot. During a walk, I found some fungi on an old tree stump with moss growing above it but not below it. I took the shot from a little bit above the fungi and had the focus ring set to about the half way point between the maximum and minimum focus settings. When I saw that the background, with all

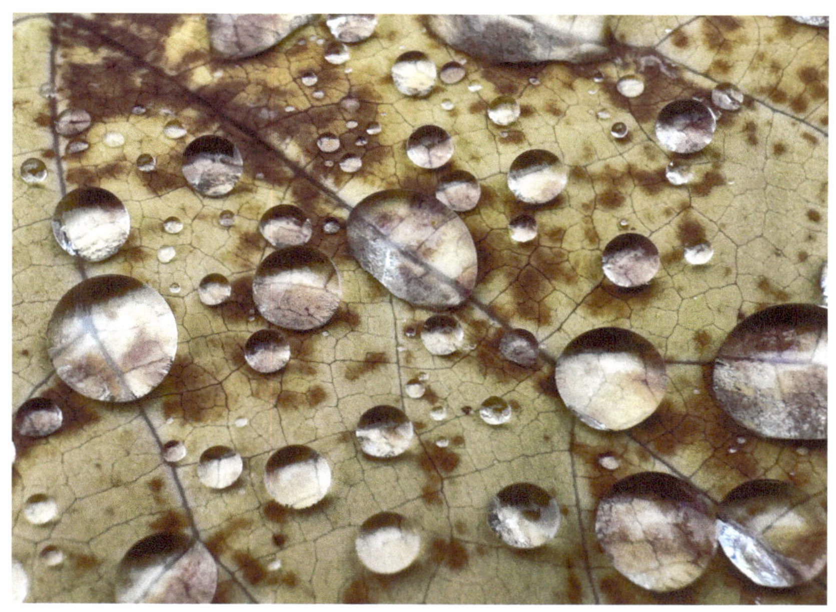

Rain drops on a leaf captured with an iPhone 15 Pro Max in Macro Mode.

the moss in the frame, was drawing my eyes away from the fungi, I adjusted the ring to a closer focus distance, moved the iPhone in and took another shot. Cropping the photo would have a similar effect but you wouldn't have a full resolution file.

When Apple introduced the iPhone 13 Pro, I was excited to see they added macro functionality to the native Camera app, but I was skeptical as to how well it would do. Since I didn't upgrade from the 12 Pro until the 14 Pro came out, I had no experience with this macro feature but when I finally got to try it, I have to say it was okay for me at best. The images looked a little over processed for my liking, which is a complaint from a lot of people about phone cameras in general. I compared a shot of the same thing taken with the macro function of the Apple Camera with a shot taken with a lens attached and I much preferred the latter version better (refer to the images on page 18). The Apple Camera macro just didn't have that nice depth of field you get with a lens, and that depth of field really helps to isolate the subject and can also assist with decluttering the image.

It may be a personal preference but I find the cluttered background of a macro photo takes too much away from the subject. If you feel the same way, be sure to examine the scene and look for ways to reduce the clutter.

ABSTRACT ART WITH MACRO

I've spent the whole time in this book telling you how to get sharp, focused photos with a macro lens, but for this segment I want you to throw that all away. But just for this segment. And why would I ask you to do that? To create art.

This will be the easiest technique to master and could yield some very interesting results for you because all you have to do is take a blurry photo. It sounds so wrong but perhaps you've already taken one by accident. I know I have and I've been pleasantly surprised by what I captured. You see, a completely blurred out photo could be considered a form of abstract art. Abstract is basically some form of visual art that doesn't represent reality but rather uses shapes, colours and textures to achieve its intended effect.

A blurry photograph is just shapes and colours, and quite possibly textures. One could look at a blurry macro photo and wonder what it is, or just get lost in the jumbled maze of bokeh. You can get an abstract image by simply moving away from your subject until it is well out of focus or photograph a scene as you normally would but with the macro lens attached, which would give you an obviously blurred image.

There's an opportunity to practice other photographic techniques here too, such as motion blur. You will already have the blur, all you need is motion. With your camera app, whether it's the Apple Camera or your favourite third-party app, on Auto, start panning the iPhone and while you're in motion, tap the shutter. Faster camera movement will result in more blur while less movement will obviously produce the opposite.

If you want more motion blur or just the ability to get the shot with a slower panning action, go to the manual setting on your third-party app and set the shutter speed to something like 1/15th of a second. The ISO should compensate to give you a well exposed photo so this process shouldn't be too difficult to work with.

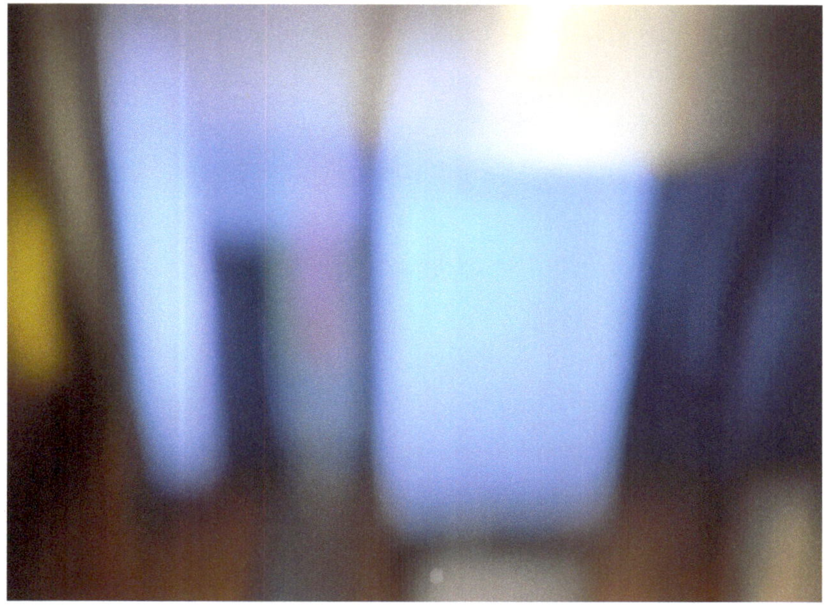

My computer screen taken while panning the camera downward.

You can get a "tunnel" effect by using that slower shutter speed and tapping the shutter while you quickly approach your subject. To ensure the centre of the frame contains exactly what you want, start close to the subject and move away while taking the shot.

I've always considered abstract art to be best displayed at a larger size, so while it will be fun to play around with the carefree concept of taking blurry photos, consider where they will be displayed, whether it's just on a social outlet like Flickr, Instagram or Glass, or in print on the wall. I believe the smaller the image is intended to be, the less "busy" the composition should be, but it's completely subjective and you have the freedom to create it as you please.

SHOOTING MACRO VIDEO

Macro video is something we don't often think of doing but when you try it and get a good result, you end up with something really cool. If you're not big on shooting video on your iPhone, don't worry, you don't need any special skills or extra apps for this stuff, it can all be done with the Apple Camera app. The tricky part is holding the iPhone still.

I think the most popular subjects for macro video will be insects and flowers. I'll cover those two topics here for now but by all means, use your imagination and find other things to record.

The nice thing about capturing insects on video is that we get a much better look at how they move about, or even fly if they have that ability. I would suggest that any time you take a video of an insect, shoot it in Slow Motion, with the Slo-Mo setting in the Camera app.

In Slo-Mo, you can record at 120 frames per second (fps) or at 240 fps. Something to remember is that 240 fps will require more light than 120 because that frame rate requires a faster shutter speed for each frame. If there isn't enough light, the video footage shot at 240 fps will be darker and it might not be useable.

I will use 240 fps whenever possible because it gives the best result for a Slo-Mo video. The frame rate settings are found in the Settings app under Camera. While you're there, you can choose the resolution for shooting video too. As you will see in the screenshot, there are a few different formats to choose from. Shooting in 4K will give you room to crop down and still allow for an output of 1080p.

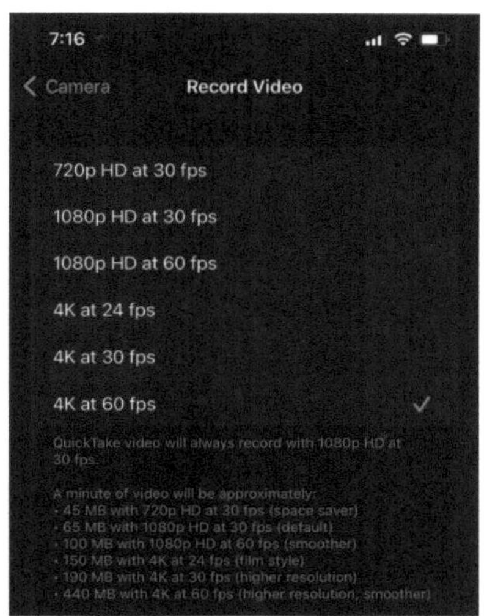

Resolution and frame rate setting for the iPhone's video camera.

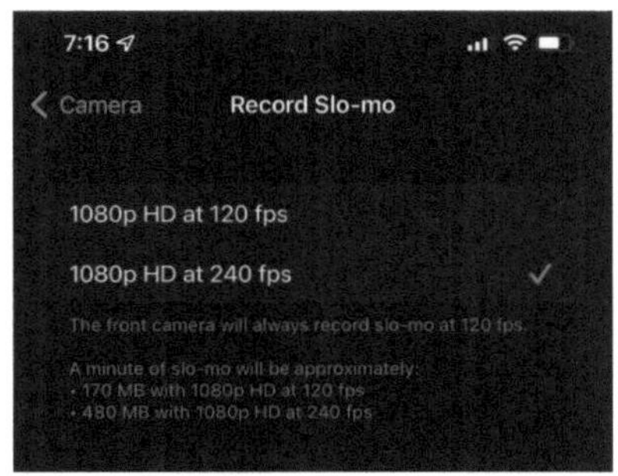

The two speeds available for Slo-Mo.

One of my favourite macro videos I've shot is that of a bee flying from one flower to another. When I recorded the bee, it was a bright, sunny day so I was able to capture it at 240 fps. When the bee took flight, you can see the wings in action. Tap here or hold your camera over the QR code to see the video. I used my Struman Optics Macro Lens to record it and the bee was so fast when it went from one

Scan to see a bee in Slo-Mo.

flower to the next that I not only lost it in the frame but also lost focus on it. Had I not used Slo-Mo, the experience would have lasted barely a second or two. Ants are another favourite subject of mine for macro. With a macro lens on your iPhone, losing focus can happen easily, so be prepared to tap the screen on the subject to regain focus so you can keep recording. You'll find that if you haven't done any macro video before, you will likely get a few blurry videos at the beginning. I know I did, but once you get to know how to maneuver the camera, you should get some better results in short order. Sometimes ants can be a little predictive if you watch them enough, especially when they're on a flower. When I've recorded them they seemed to go from the front side to the back side and around to the front side again

Scan to see an ant in Slo-Mo.

and they tend to stay on the same flower longer than bees. Slo-Mo video takes something that lasts a very short amount of time and allows you to watch it over a longer period, but what about doing the opposite? Can we shoot something over a longer period of time and watch it in a short amount of time? We sure can, and it's called a time-lapse.

In the iPhone's Camera app, there's the mode selector where you can choose which type of camera function you want to use. Along with Photo, you have Portrait and Pano to the right, and to the left of Photo is Video, Slo-Mo, and Time-Lapse. The way the iPhone records a time-lapse is really clever because it doesn't work the way you think it does. Rather than shoot at a regular frame rate, like Video or Slo-Mo, it use a technique called "dynamically selected intervals" where the camera shoots at 2 fps to start, then begins to drop frames over time to fit the whole video into a 20 to 40 second timeframe depending on the length of recording time. There's more to it than that but it's just another example of Apple's ingenuity with their camera systems.

Since time-lapse videos are recordings of things that change over a long period of time, what could we record with a macro lens that would be interesting enough as a time-lapse? The first thing that comes to mind is a melting ice cube, but there are many possibilities for this technique. Maybe you have a flowering house plant where the blooms open each morning, as long as they're small enough to get a close shot of them. Try setting up your iPhone next to some bubbles, either in the kitchen sink or just put a drop of dish soap in a glass and run some water in it to create a bubbly landscape and record them as they slowly fizzle away. If you live in a place where you get snow in the winter, set your iPhone up to record the snow as it

Scan to see a Timelapse
of bubbles popping.

melts.

A time-lapse can be recorded over a few minutes or you can let it go for hours. You can set up your iPhone to capture the growing process of a newly seeded plant over the course of a day and watch the video to see the seedling pop out of the soil right before your eyes. If you want to do a long time-lapse like that, I'd suggest you set it up on a tripod near an electrical outlet so you can keep it plugged in to charge, or at the very least, connect it to some sort of portable charging device.

Finally, when shooting macro video, be mindful of your light source. If the sun is your source of light, remember that it moves as the day goes on, and that may have a profound effect on your video's outcome.

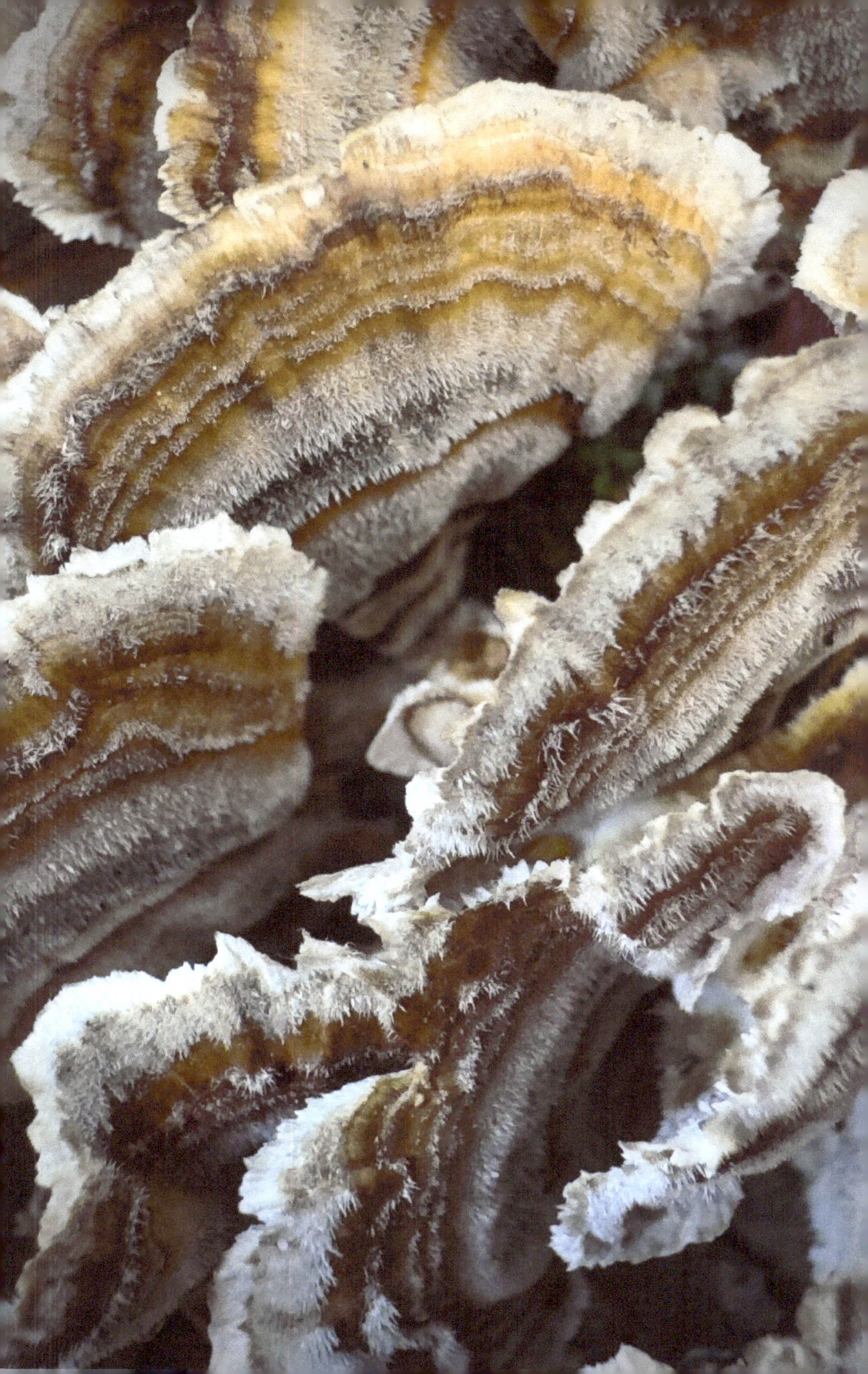

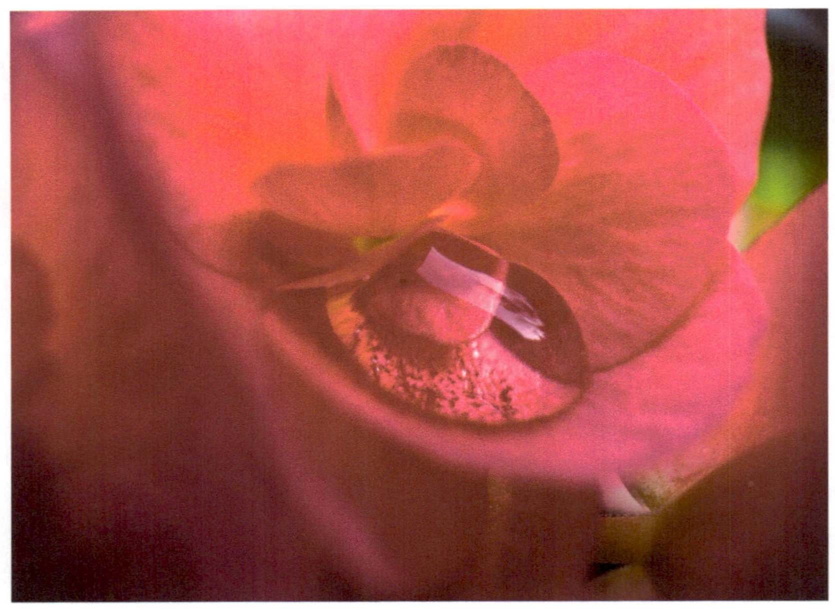

Chapter 8 - Editing

If you were to edit photos back in the days before digital photography, you would be going through a number of images, either in the form of slides, negatives, or prints, to figure out which ones you want to keep or find a specific use for, and that was the editing process. Now, in the digital age, especially since the invention of programs like Photoshop, etc., editing has evolved from merely sorting images into processing image files and altering them from their original state. Photo editing is a form of art in itself that many people struggle with in their photography. Admittedly, the newer iPhones on the market today are taking photos so well that oftentimes editing just isn't necessary. I find that the dynamic range when shooting in JPG, HEIC or ProRAW is so good that shadows and highlights rarely need much correction at all.

However, I'm sure you've heard of the term "photographic style". Style comes in different ways, some of which are subject matter, technical processes, or editing. Over the years I've developed a style based on my editing. I can apply the same basic adjustments to just about any photo and when I scroll through my Instagram feed, the images all seem to have a similar look to them. There are so many different ways to edit photos because each one of us has our own taste or preference, so I couldn't cover too many without it being a book all of its own, but I'll go over some things that I hope you find useful.

There are a plethora of editing apps available for the iPhone, and in recent years, editing on the iPad has become more popular. You can use the editing functions in Photos that comes with your device or you can get the popular iPhone apps like Snapseed, Lightroom Mobile or Darkroom to name a few, and all of which are available on the iPad.

GENERAL TIPS

If you're an editing guru, you may want to skip this section but if you're new at it, these general tips may get you on your way. I suppose these tips can be applied to photos in general, but I'll see if I can think of some that may be more relevant to macro images, and I will expand on some of them further as we go.

A great looking photo usually starts with one that has been captured just right, whether the subject itself is something remarkable, or the focus and exposure are perfect. Having a good image to start with makes the editing process much easier and a more enjoyable experience.

I don't really have a "do and don't" list because art is subjective, but in my experience with editing, one thing I learned many years ago from Michael McLuhan, a Master of the Photographic Arts, was to prevent over-sharpening the image. I had asked for his thoughts on a photo that I had printed - 11 x 14 if I recall - and immediately, without hesitation, he said it

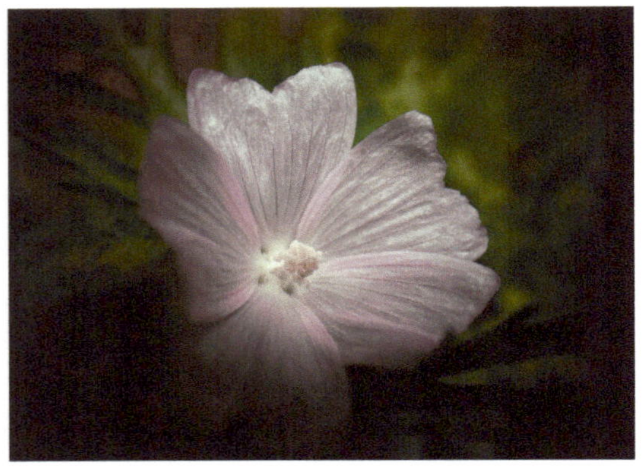

The edit of a flower portraying a darker mood.

was over-sharpened. When I realized what he meant by that, and after reviewing the photo, the look of that little anomaly has stayed with me, and sharpening a photo is something I now do very carefully. More on sharpening shortly.

When adjusting for highlights and shadows, be mindful of how it affects the rest of the photo. I think the way these two parts of an image are adjusted can

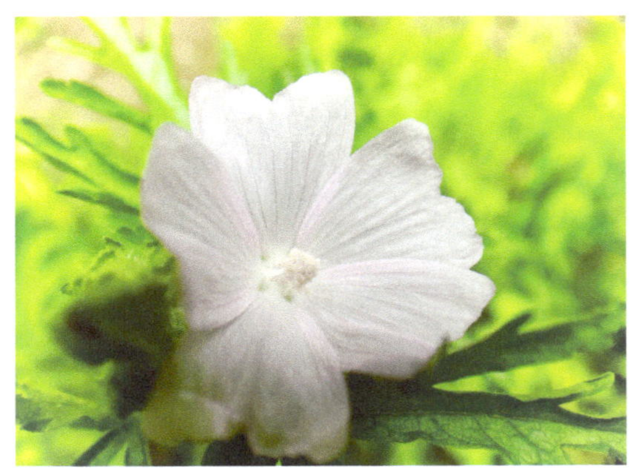

The same image file edited to portray a lighter mood.

certainly determine the mood in the end, and by mood, I mean the "feeling" the viewer gets when looking at it. A photo that's been edited to give it a darker look with more emphasis on the shadow areas may tend to portray a solemn mood or one of misery, given the right subject of course. Darker images are sometimes called low key photos, but images with more bright, or even white areas are high key photos. When you put the emphasis on the lighter areas of a photo, you may experience a happier mood when viewing it.

Highlights and shadows can be over-processed to the point where there is no detail left in those parts of the photo, and this can certainly be intentional, but be mindful of that when making your adjustments.

So, in general, editing, in the simplest form, is basically starting with a decent photo, where sharpening too much can ruin it, and the state of the highlights and shadows can determine the mood portrayed in the image or perhaps, like over-sharpening, can also ruin it. I'm going to touch more on sharpening, and as we go through some of the other types of edits, highlights and shadows will undoubtedly be a part of the topic. Also, one of the best practices in editing, especially if you're new to it all, is when you are adjusting the sliders in your app of choice, move them from one end of its scale to the other. This will allow you to see what it does and you'll have a better idea of where to leave the adjustment. I've found over the years that with most adjustments you don't need to go overboard with the sliders. Keep the moves subtle. But again, it's subjective.

SHARPENING

It's always good to start with a sharp photo right from the beginning but doing some additional sharpening on a macro photo can enhance certain parts of it just enough to draw the viewer's eye to the right spot. I've stated it earlier but it's worth mentioning yet again that a good, sharp macro photo can be hard to get, and if you don't have some amount of sharpness in the image to start with, well, you just can't sharpen a blurry photo. Macro photos of incests or very finely detailed plant life, like moss, may have a small portion of it in sharp focus, but that sharp focus can be improved to enhance the viewing experience. Sharpening can be done in any editing app with a simple Sharpening slider like the one found in the edit suite of Photos, or with more advanced tools like those in Lightroom Mobile where you have Sharpening, Radius, Detail and Masking. In most cases, and for most people, the Sharpening slider alone will probably be enough to do the trick, but for those who want to

The sharpening adjustments found in Lightroom Mobile.

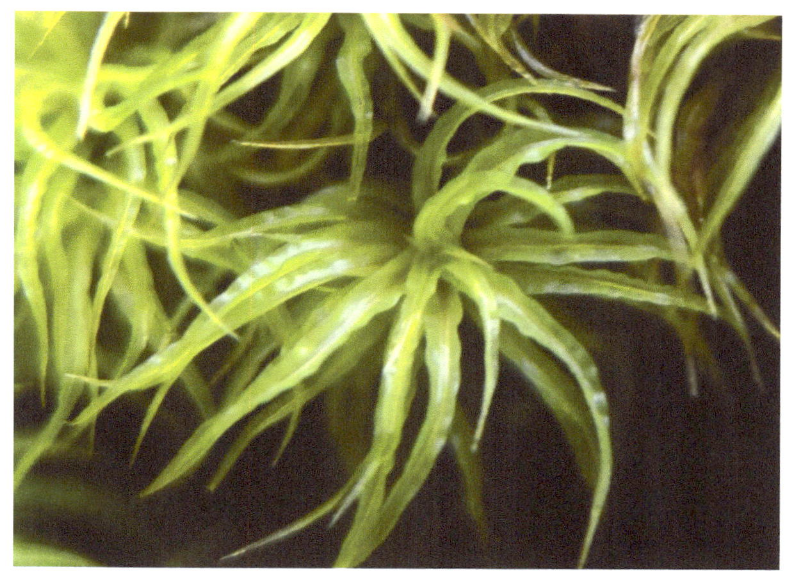

A close up of moss that hasn't been sharpened.

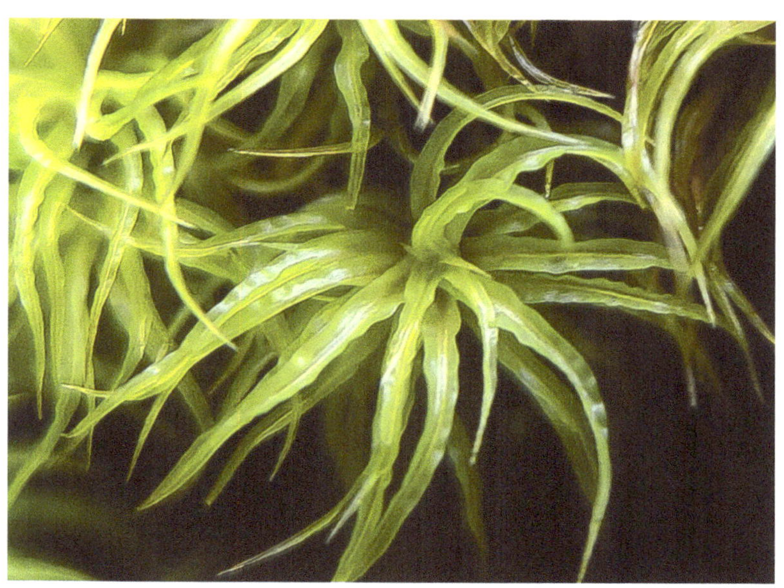

The image with sharpening completed.

learn more about the other, more complex tools of sharpening, let's do a quick review of the ones found in Lightroom Mobile. It should be noted that Lr Mobile is free to use with in-app purchases, which are the subscription plans available that give you access to Adobe's Creative Cloud as well as some extra tools in the app. The ones we're looking at here are part of the free version.

Sharpening: This slider controls the amount of enhancement that gets applied to the edges.

Radius: This slider controls how wide the edge is where the sharpening is applied. If a photo has a lot of edge detail, like a macro photo of moss, a smaller number on the Radius slider will work better, and conversely, a photo with less detail, like a simple flower petal, can handle a larger value.

Detail: This slider controls how much sharpening is applied to the edges that contain more detail. This one works in reverse compared to the Radius slider in that a lower value will sharpen larger edges and a larger value on the scale will affect areas of finer detail. A word of caution with this slider though: be careful with the higher values because since it affects the finer areas of detail, it also affects any noise in the image. The last thing you want to do is enhance the noise.

Masking: This slider allows the sharpening to affect the whole image when it is set at zero, or, as you move it to a higher value, it only applies the sharpening to more detailed areas.

Two very helpful tips to remember when sharpening: 1) zoom in on the area you are working on and 2) tap and hold on the image before moving a slider. This will give you the best view of how these tools are affecting the image, plus you will easily see if you are over-sharpening.

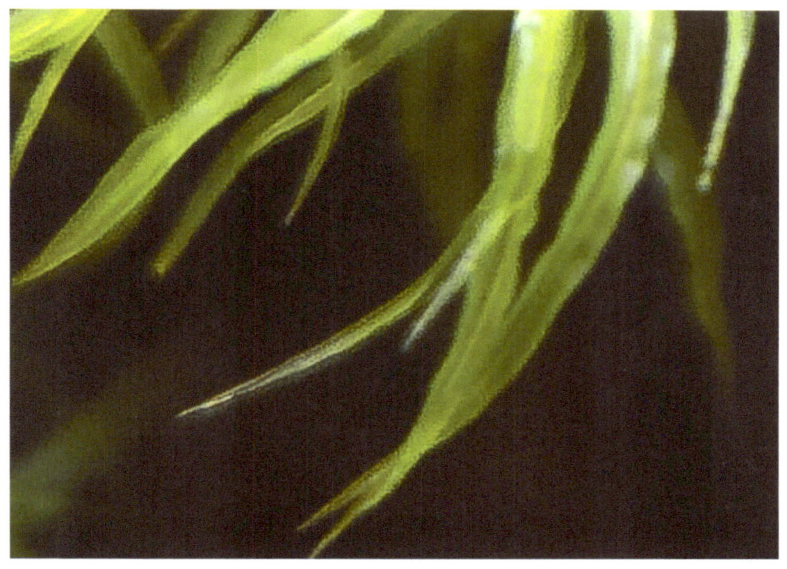

A close look at the image sharpened, but it has a lot of noise.

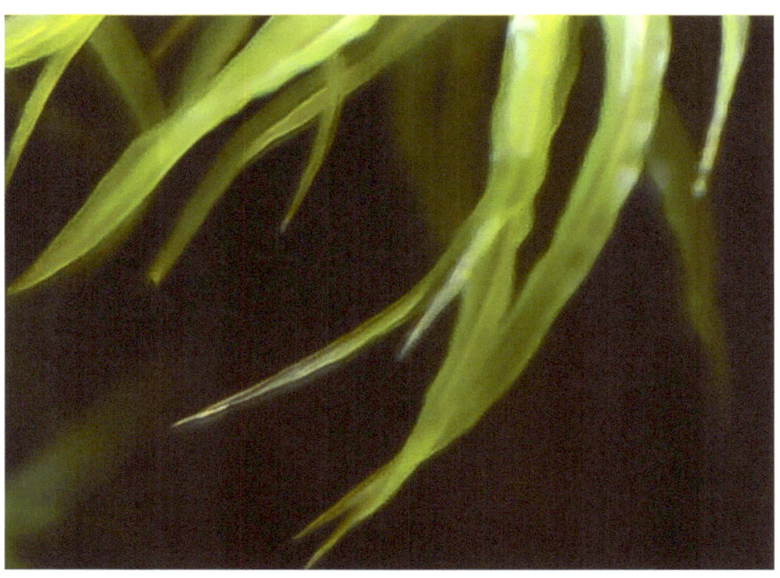

The sharpened image with Noise Reduction applied.

CROPPING

The iPhone, when held horizontally, takes a photo in a 4:3 aspect ratio, whereby the aspect ratio is the ratio between the width and height of the photo. Aspect ratio also applies to screen shape, like on televisions and computers, and 4:3 was the ratio used on these screens before the days of high definition. HD screens are now in a ratio of 16:9, which is wider and more pleasing to the viewer. The iPhone's Camera app shoots 4:3 by default, but starting with the iPhone XS we've been able to change the aspect ratio to 16:9 to produce a wider shot at the point of capture. Prior to the XS, the Camera app didn't have the ability to shoot photos in 16:9 but many third-party camera apps had that feature available.

In photography, you may come across an image that just doesn't look proper in a 4:3 ratio, so what do we do? We crop it to get rid of any unwanted elements in the frame. Cropping a photo in digital photography is essentially the same as taking a print and cutting parts of it away, generally in straight sections parallel to the original edge of the print. You may be wondering how you could have unwanted elements in a macro photo, but believe me, it can happen.

Since macro photos have that ever-so-small depth of field, there will be times when most of the image is blurred. In some cases, when the point of interest, or the sharpest part of the photo, takes up such a small portion of the frame, it could be a good idea to eliminate the stuff that doesn't matter. Or, maybe you can't position the camera at the optimum angle. Take this shot of a rose for instance. I wanted to get the edges of certain petals in sharp focus, so I tried different camera angles, but when I got the shot I wanted, I couldn't fill the frame with just the rose and some of the background was showing on the right. I didn't like that. I thought it drew my eyes away from the focal point of the rose which is that little curl on the petal in the central part of the frame. A simple crop off the top,

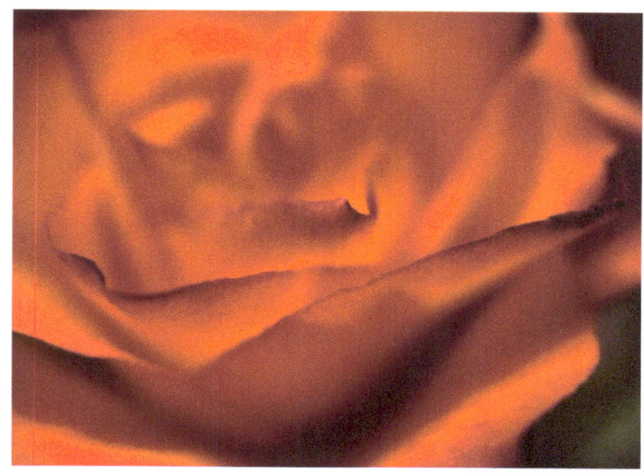

An image of a rose before cropping.

bottom, and right side at a 16:9 aspect ratio was all that was needed, and when I did the crop, I was sure to put the little curl one third of the way down from the top to abide by the rule of thirds. Now my eyes move along the edges of the petals across the lower third and

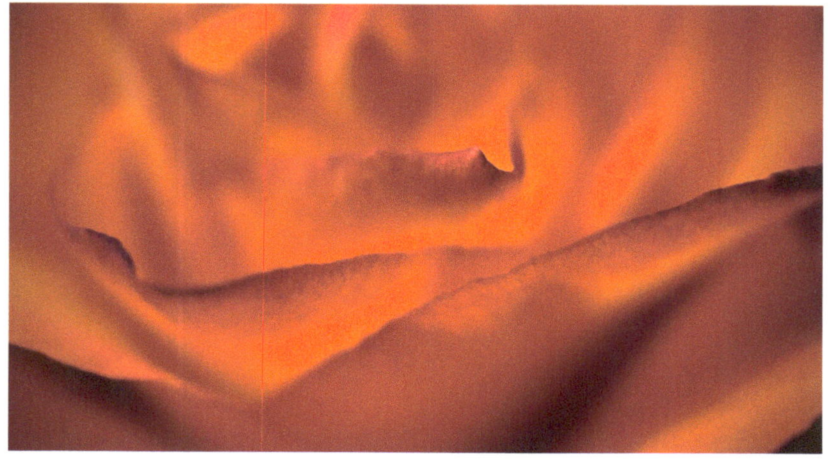

The rose after cropping.

wind up right at the little curl. Now that you've read this and looked at the image, did I succeed?

Cropping doesn't always have to create a different shape for your photo because while some photos look just fine in their original shape, they may just need a little off the edges. Other shapes are useful, however, like the square crop. Instagram made it the most popular aspect ratio for years when the platform exploded to become THE place to be for mobile photographers, but going square isn't always the best solution. It greatly depends on whether or not it works for the photo's composition.

Something that drives some photographers crazy is the fact that photo frames are rarely, if ever, made to fit a photo that is 4:3. Frames come in 5x7 (inches), 8x10 (4:5 ratio), or 11x14, but I have yet to find one that would fit a photo at the default ratio of any camera. Even DSLR photos don't fit anything but a 4x6 frame because their default ratio is 3:2. The point I'm making here is if you want to print your macro photos and frame them, you will almost certainly have to crop them. The only way to escape it is to have a

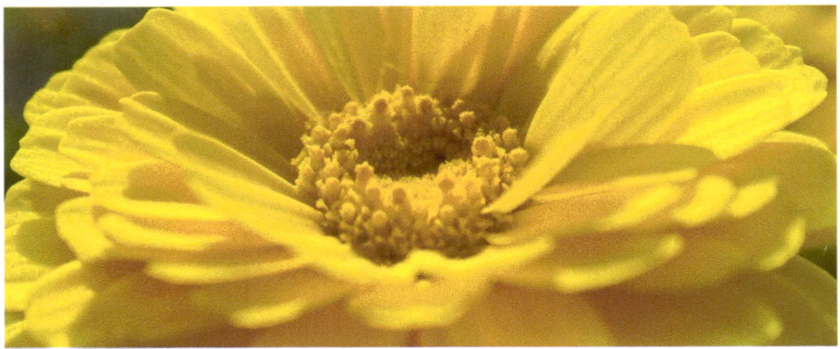

A possible panorama enlargement.

custom frame or canvas made, or have a matte cut to fit the 4:3 photo in the opening and fit the matte in a frame of your choosing.

I have aspirations of getting a macro shot enlarged to a massive size. I just need to find the right photo and who knows, maybe I've already taken it. What I have in mind is to make it a panoramic photo. I think that would be such an ironic thing to do. Generally, panoramic photos are ones of grand vistas that contain a lot of detail and keep the viewer engaged for a while as they explore the vastness of the scene. I think a macro photo enlarged in a panoramic shape would be something of a conversation piece. Look at this pano of a little bug as it walks through this flower. Now imagine it about six feet long on the wall above your sofa. Ok, that's a little big, but you get the idea. It's something different, something not many people think of doing.

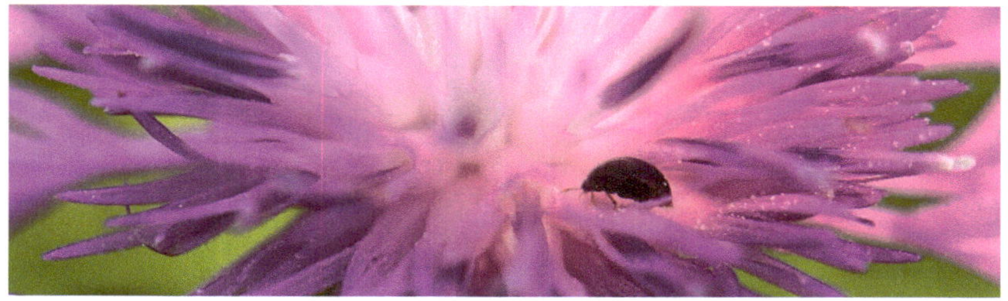

Another possible pano enlargement.

I want to cover one final, but very important point about cropping, and this applies mostly to printing your work. When you crop a photo, remember that you are chopping away precious pixels. It can't be helped, but it's a necessary evil when you want to make your composition better after the fact. So if you can, make your crop on as few edges as possible. If you can keep your photo at its original width or height, you will still have as much data to work with as you need for that print. Cutting away pixels for online viewing isn't as crucial because you can crop to any shape you desire as long as you have enough pixels left that the image doesn't need to be stretched in order to be seen. Cropping can be a large part of the creative process and can sometimes make or break a good photo.

BLACK AND WHITE

I rarely think of what a photo would look like as a black and white when I capture it, but when I'm sitting down to browse through my camera roll looking for something to edit, I may find one where I wonder what it will look like in all those shades of grey.

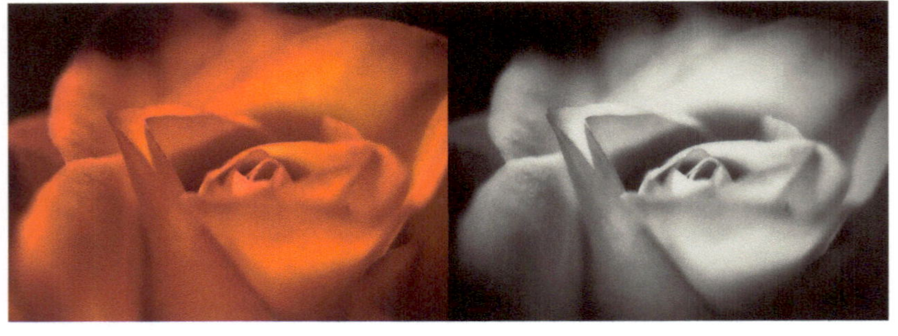

A rose in colour…   … and edited in black and white.

When I select an image to try in black and white, I look for something in the frame that could stand out when there is no colour, otherwise you have a photo that lacks interest. A monochromatic photo, like the rose pictured here, looks stunning in colour, but when you convert it to black and white and add some softness to the look, you have something with an element of mystery since you wouldn't know what colour the flower really is if the coloured version was absent.

Flowers are beautiful and it makes sense to see them in colour but do yourself a favour and try converting some of your flower shots to black and white. Macro shots can look good in colour or black and white, just like any other genre, whether it's insects, plant life, or household trinkets. Anything goes.

With an iPhone, not only can you convert an image to black and white, but you can also

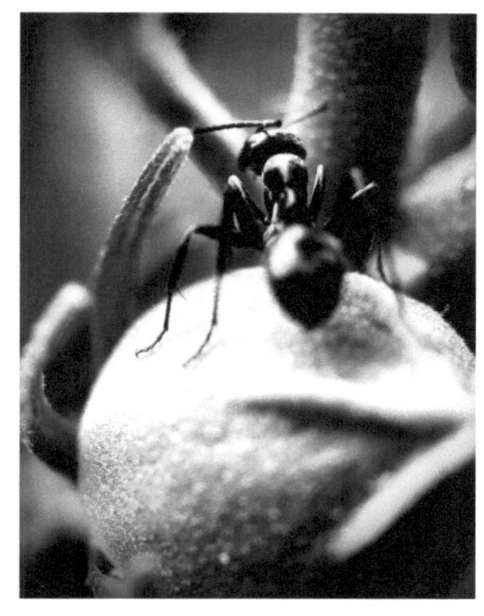

An ant in black and white.

capture it that way. Let's look at cutting to the chase with black and white image capture. While the App Store has camera apps specifically for black and white photography, I want to start with the one that comes with the phone, the Camera app.

A little known trick in the Camera app is to apply a filter to the image before you take the shot. This is a great way to know if the photo is going to look good as a black and white. There are three black and white filters in the Camera app, Mono, Silvertone and Noir. Mono is basically a desaturated image that has no other processing done to it, but Noir has some added contrast to darken the shadows and brighten the lighter parts of the photo. Silvertone looks to be somewhere in between Mono and Noir as far as contrast goes, but with more emphasis on the shadows. These filters are the same ones you find in the Edit screen of the Photos app, and even if you shoot the photo with a filter applied, you can still go into the Edit screen and either make further adjustments or tap the Revert button to turn the black and white back into a colour photo.

When editing a photo with a black and white filter applied to it, you can make almost any adjustment that Photos has to offer except those reserved for altering the colour, like Saturation, Vibrance, Temperature and Tint.

Another app that shoots in black and white is Blackie. This app has a lot of diversity with regards to how the image will look, including some of the famous black and white film looks from the pre-digital era. Blackie has an editing suite built in so you can change the look of the image further, either before you shoot or afterwards. Part of the editing suite is a series of coloured filters that were often used when shooting black and white film. The way these filters work is interesting. For instance, if you use a green filter,

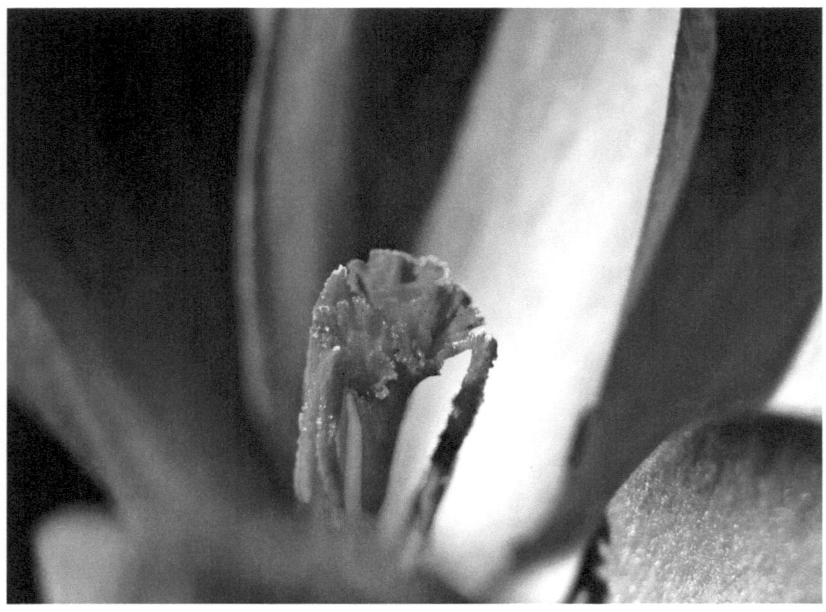

A colourful purple Crocus takes on a different mood
when edited in black and white.

anything that's green in the frame, like grass or leaves, will get lighter while anything that is green's complimentary colour in the colour wheel, will get darker. The same theory will apply to any coloured filter.

I realize I didn't mention much on the subject of macro here, but black and white can make your macro photos interesting and they'll be different than what most people would expect in a macro.

FOCUS STACKING

This section is quite advanced in nature and may only appeal to those who have the software on their computers required to perform the task of focus stacking. The purpose of this type of edit is to defeat that barrier I've mentioned numerous times throughout this book, the shallow depth of field. Focus stacking requires a number of exposures, perhaps dozens, all taken at different focal points in order to make the entire subject sharp. In my experience with doing this, there's only one proper way to do it with any level of success, and that is to use a camera app that has the ability to shoot enough photos in one burst to build a good stack. The only app that I'm aware of is CameraPixels, which comes in both a free and paid version. The difference? The free

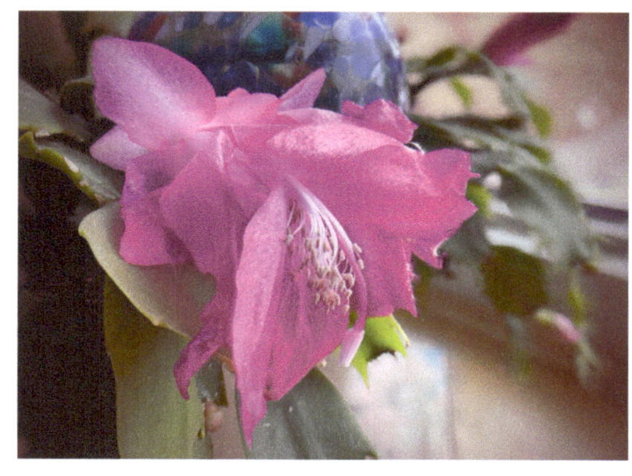

A focus stacked Christmas Cactus bloom.

version only allows image capture up to 3.1 MP, which is about 1/4 the resolution of the iPhone's 12 MP sensor. CameraPixels Lite has all the functionality of the Pro version so you can certainly try it out to see if focus stacking is something you want to do and if it is, it's well worth the upgrade to Pro. In the Canadian App Store, that's a $6.99 upgrade and well worth it for doing this type of work at full resolution.

I'm sure you are asking why you couldn't just use Burst Mode to do this. Well, you have to change the focus as you shoot, not move the camera back and forth. Moving the camera back and forth changes the size of your subject in the frame. Remember earlier when I talked about how a macro lens really accentuates camera movement? It just isn't a practical method for macro focus stacking.

Where CameraPixels excels is with its Focus Bracketing feature. This allows the camera to capture multiple frames in increments of five from 5 up to 100. With each photo captured, the camera changes the focus as it goes through the focal range and you can set where the minimum and maximum focus points are based on a percentage of the total focal range. For macro, you need to have the minimum set to 0% and the maximum set to 100%. If you end up with images

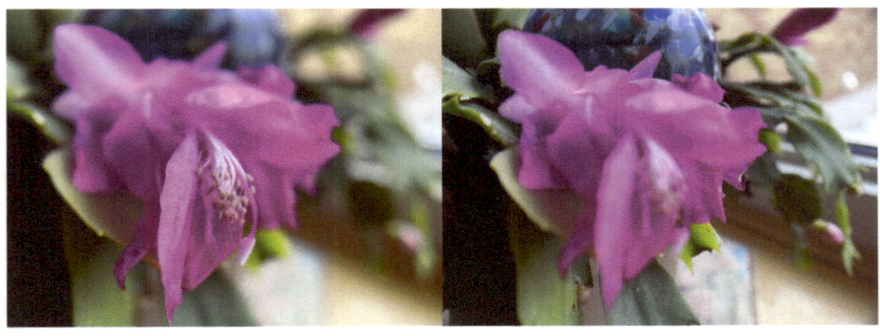

The nearest point of focus.The furthest point of focus.

outside of your intended range of focus, you can eliminate them from the processing stage. This technique will definitely require a tripod because as the app automatically adjusts the focus to the next point, you want the camera to be perfectly still. The more images you capture in the process, the finer the focus adjustments, and the better

Scan to see how CameraPixels went through the focal range.

chance the focus stacking software has to create a wonderfully sharp macro photo with the whole subject in focus.

Of course, you can do all the photographic adjustments with the camera before the shot. You can take manual control of things like white balance, ISO, shutter speed and even exposure compensation. For what we're doing here, I recommend positioning the camera so the minimum focus is at the closest part of the subject.

Something to keep in mind when shooting with a macro lens, in my case I used the Moment lens here, is that as you go through the complete range of focus, the subject will look slightly smaller at the furthest point of focus than it does at the nearest point. This is called focus breathing and it's caused by the change in the angle of view of the lens as it goes through the various focal lengths used in the shot sequence. So, you may want to compose your shot with just a tiny bit of extra room surrounding your subject because, as you'll see, when the focus stacking software is finished processing all the images, the output will be a sharp image that is the same size as the smallest usable portion. The rest of the parts are downscaled to match it because you can always scale down without losing quality, but not up.

The software that I use on my Mac is Affinity Photo which is also available on the iPad. It's very much like Photoshop but much less expensive to buy. Affinity Photo has a feature called Focus Merge, which is the focus stacking part of the program. I should note here that it might be best to transfer any photos that you want to merge together over to your computer before working with Affinity. The easiest thing to do is to put them in a folder right on your desktop for easy access. However, if you have a Mac or an iPad where your pictures sync in Photos, this isn't necessary as Affinity can get them from the Photos app.

In Affinity, under the File menu is a series of functions and you will see "New Focus Merge…". When you click on this, a small dialogue box will open with some buttons at the bottom. Click "Add" to

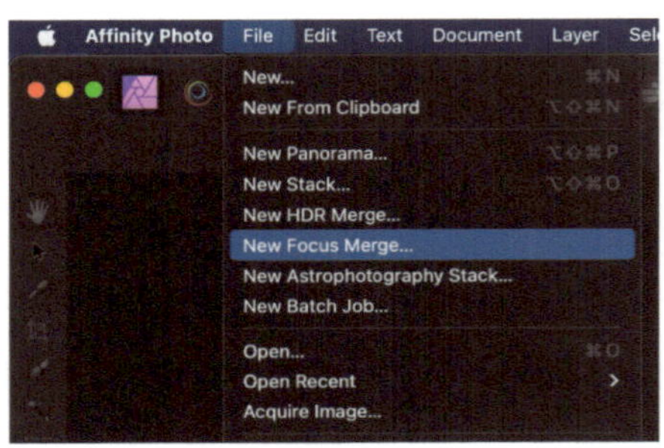

Starting a New Focus Merge process in Affinity Photo.

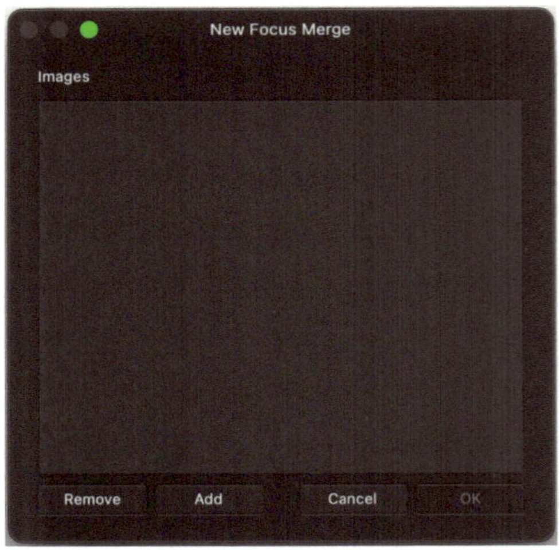

In Affinity Photo, this will be where you add your images taken from CameraPixels with the focus bracketing feature.

bring up a file browser and navigate to the folder where your photos are stored, then select all the photos taken in the Focus Bracket in CameraPixels. Once the images are selected, click "OK" and watch the magic happen.

Affinity will go through a series of processes and you'll see some strange things happen on the screen, but the end product is a nice, fully focused macro subject that would not be possible any other way when using an attachment lens on the iPhone. Once you have exported your stacked image, you can continue to edit it as you would any other image. To my knowledge, there is no app available that can perform the stacking process on the iPhone so this is definitely a desktop or iPad edit.

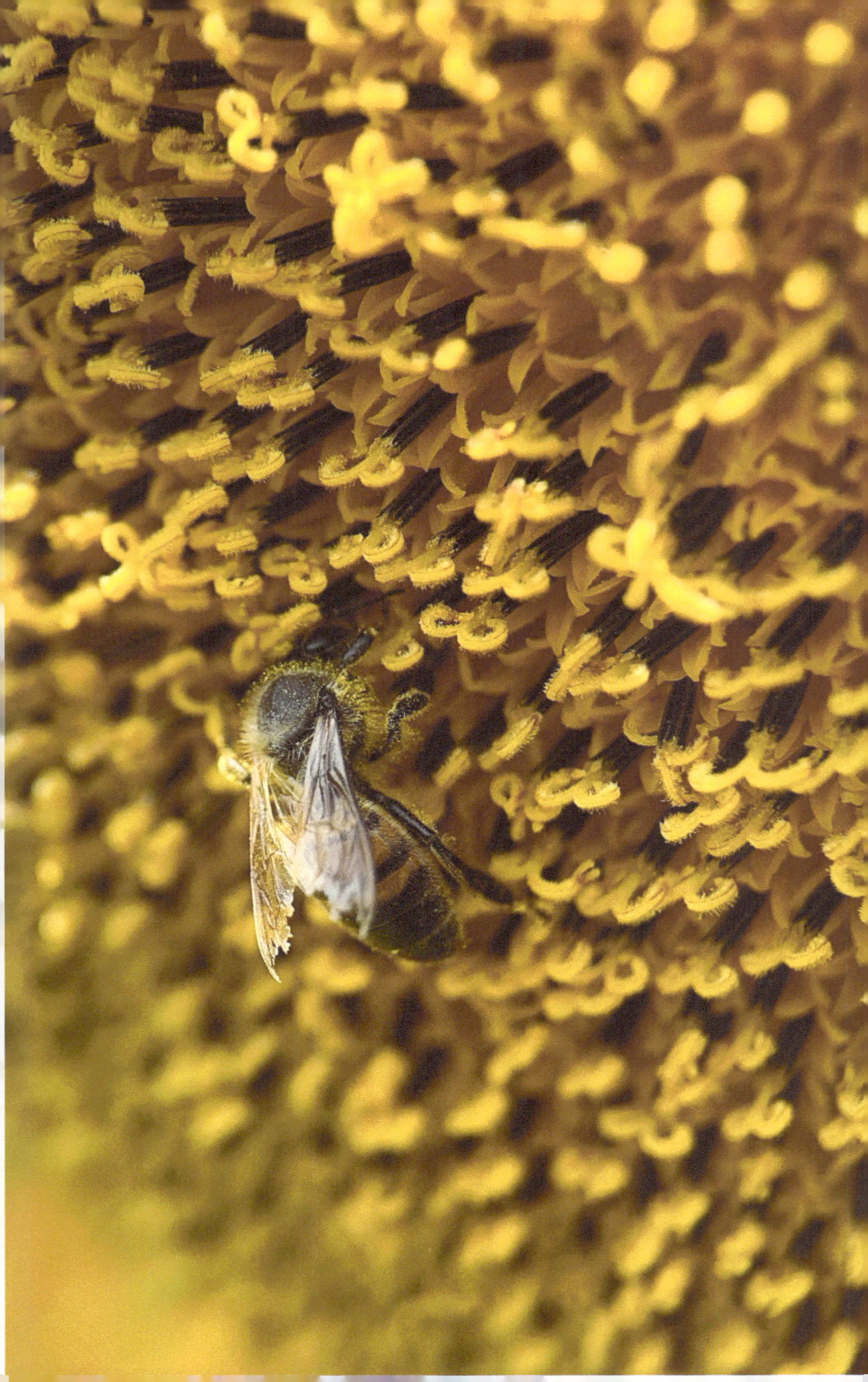

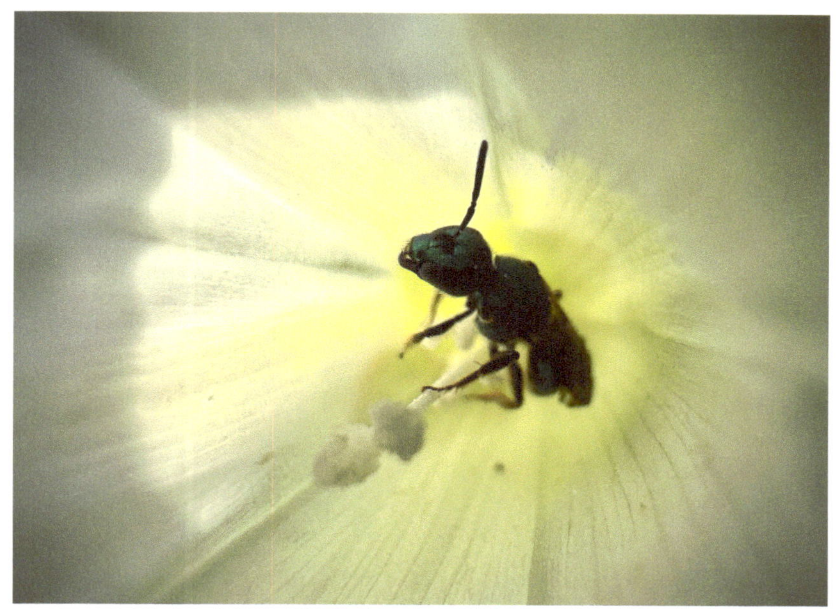

Conclusion and Final Thoughts

Macro photography is a popular genre in the world of art, and it existed long before the iPhone, which along with smartphones in general, have not only allowed macro to become even more popular, but they've allowed more people access to the tools needed to enjoy the craft. The cost of doing macro work is much less for mobile photographers than for those who shoot with traditional cameras.

There are many things I could have written about in this book that are pertinent to macro photography with an iPhone, but I think this is a good start and my hope is that it will ignite a creative spark in you to think of other ways to explore the tiny world around you. The absolute best advice I could offer you is this: immerse yourself in the moment. Look at what you're about to photograph for a few minutes to see what you can learn from it. Observe it, try to see as many details as you can before getting your iPhone out, and think about how you want to approach your subject. Then… put your lens on the phone and go to work. This is when you will be blown away by what you see on the screen.

The view through that little lens, the intricate details you see, perhaps for the first time, is the most satisfying part of the whole macro experience. Learn from it so you can tell your story to others. I think you will find a whole new appreciation for the smaller things in this world.

Photography, like anything else, is constantly changing. To see where it is now compared to how it started is mind blowing. Macro photography is evolving too, and in the time I spent writing this book, I've seen a few changes happen in the iPhone space. The Pro iPhones now have a macro feature, we have 48MP sensors, and more lens companies have emerged with their own macro (and other) lens offerings.

iPhones get better with every release, but I can tell you with the utmost assurance, you don't need the latest and greatest to do macro photography. It all starts behind the camera, with you, the photographer. You can instil the emotion or the story into the photograph. There are many ways to get your story out there, the easiest being a platform like Instagram or Glass, etc., but be creative in doing so. Experiment with how you show your work. I like to create videos with a mix of stills and video footage set to music. I find this to be a great exercise in seeing how my art has evolved over the years, and by art, I not only mean my photography, but my video skills and the efforts I put into post processing and multimedia work.

Creating memories is what this is all about. You can sit and watch an insect as it meanders its way over a mass of fungi on an old tree stump, or you can join it in its journey by getting up close for a more detailed look that you can come back to for years to come. The same applies to anything you can see through that macro lens. These are things you would miss just walking by. Thinking about that. Can you imagine what you've missed today alone? I know it isn't practical to think that way I suppose, but I guess I just want to get you thinking about macro and what is possible with it.

Take your shot. Create your art. Tell your story.

Acknowledgments

I have so much to be thankful for in my life. First and foremost, I thank God for His amazing creations and for the means to capture them.

Second only to God, I thank my wife, Gail. Thank you for your love, patience, support and understanding when it comes to my desire to practice photography. Especially for the time it took me to write this book. I love you dearly.

My parents have always encouraged me in all that I do. Thank you for that encouragement. You are my heroes in this world, and I dedicate this book to you.

I have so many people to thank for their support and friendship in my photographic life. Everyone, from the friends I have locally to those who I know all around the world, you are all an inspiration to me and I thank you for your encouragement. The following will not be in any order because I place everyone in the same spot in my heart.

My podcasting ventures would not be possible without the crew from Tiny Shutter. Marc Sadowski, Matt Hoffman, Joseph Ferreira, and Dave Podnar, thank you for your friendships and for introducing me to a medium where I can talk about this stuff and bring my passion for iPhoneography to the world.

Don Komarechka, yes, the snowflake guy, you've been a big influence to me for macro photography. The iPhone is not your primary tool for macro work, but the concepts you bring forth and the images you show are truly inspiring and there is so much to learn from your techniques. Thank you for your brilliant mind.

It was Jack Hollingsworth who helped me find my drive to jump into mobile photography with both feet, and that was before we became friends. Jack, you inspire me to become a better photographer by doing something I rarely think about, and that is exploring the emotional side of the medium. Thank you for your thoughtfulness, advice, and friendship. I can't wait to get out and shoot alongside you someday.

Meri Walker, you have taught me so much, not only as an artist, but as a person. You gave me the strength and encouragement I needed to embark on my podcasting adventure. Thank you for your infectious resilience, your kindness, and your friendship.

Mike James, your teaching skills are like no one I've seen before. You have such a systematic way of instructing people with your courses that I can't imagine why anyone wouldn't want to learn from you. I also want to thank you for pushing me to make this book available in print when I thought digital was the only way to go and for your remarkable editing skills. You make me sound like I know what I'm talking about.

Shayne Mostyn, we've gone from "Who the hell is that guy?" to "Hey, we doing a livestream on the weekend?" Thank you for your friendship and the advice when I ask for it. We may be 16,000 km from each other but it's nice to know we always have each other's back and it seems like it's just a stone's throw away at times.

The mobile photography community is global. I know so many great artists that I simply couldn't name them all. Some who come to mind are - in alphabetical order - Andy Butler, Andy Green, Anil Dave, Brendan Ó Sé, Cielo De La Paz, Chris Feichtner, Christopher Cohen, Dale Lotherington, David Addison, Elaine Taylor, Glen Mulcahy, Ithalu Dominguez, Jefferson Graham, Jo Bradford, Joanne

Carter, Mario Tomiak, Mark Deaves, Mike Goin, Neill Barham, Nicki Fitz-Gerald, Paul Yan, Ralph Mayhew, Reece Boyd, Rick Sammon, Rob Layton, Ron Duvall, Scott Baker, Scott Bourne, Tim Bingham, and the list goes on. If you haven't seen their work, look them up as I know you'll be inspired.

There are some folks who make great apps and products that we as mobile photographers can use in our macro adventures. There are many great macro lens makers out there, but I personally have to thank Reeflex, Struman Optics, Moment and ShiftCam for the quality lenses I've had the pleasure of using. I honestly can't say I have a favourite brand because they are all brilliant products.

The team at Reeflex, Joshua Salomone, Salvatore De Angelis, and Mattia Marvardi have created a camera app that I find a pleasure to use with its intuitive design giving me great results. Since I started writing this book, they've released two more camera apps in ReeXpose and ReeHeld, both niche products that I love using. Thank you Reeflex for these great camera apps that will always be present on my iPhone and thank you for your support.

I would be remiss if I didn't thank Riley Arthur, whom I interviewed on my podcast, for planting the seed and unknowingly convincing me to write this book. Riley, you said I should, and had you not said it, I wouldn't have put any thought to it and no one would be reading these words right now. Thank you for your confidence and belief in me.

Finally, I'd like to thank you, the reader, for taking the time to explore the macro world with me. You are a big part of why I do what I do with my camera.

God Bless you all.

About the Author

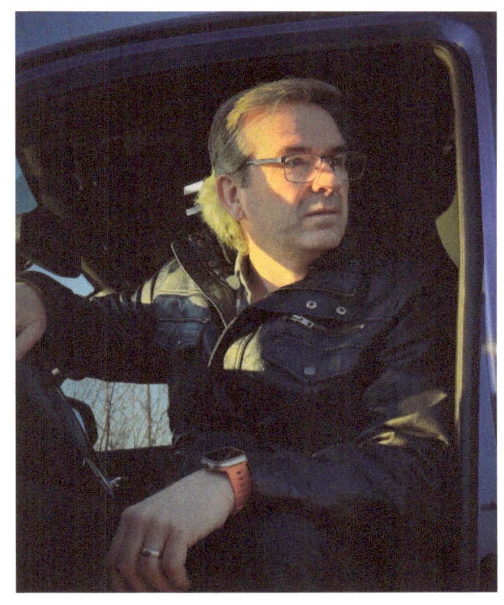

Greg McMillan has been a photography enthusiast for most of his life, and since 2016 has been shooting solely with an iPhone. All of his work is done in the mobile photography space - shooting, editing, sharing. It's only a rare occasion where he'll edit on a desktop. The images in this book go back as far as July 2016, when Greg first tried macro work, and have been taken with six different versions of the iPhone.

Greg's passion for iPhone photography has led him to meet (albeit online) so many great people from all over the world, even the who's who in the mobile photography space. A few years ago he became a co-host on the Tiny Shutter podcast, which was the longest running podcast dedicated solely to iPhone photography, that ran for almost 9 years. That experience allowed him to start his own show in January 2019 called The Artful iPhoneography Interviews. He started it as a companion to an online community he hosted for iPhoneographers aptly named The Artful iPhoneography Community.

Tiny Shutter ceased regular production, so Greg is carrying the torch on his newly named show called The iPhoneography Podcast where he and his Tiny Shutter alumni co-host Dave Podnar bring you a bi-weekly podcast about all things iPhoneography. They talk about everything from news items to iPhones to apps. You name it, they'll cover it. In addition to Greg's show, The David Addison Show was added under the iPhoneography Podcast banner for a short time. David, a YouTube creator growing in popularity, had joined the network to bring more iPhoneography-related content in the form of interviews, reviews, and how-to's.

Greg has worked in the printing industry for over 40 years and resides in Owen Sound, Ontario, Canada with his wife, Gail. Although there are many places in the world that offer better photo opportunities, he wouldn't trade living in the area for anything. He says, "We have almost everything within a couple of hours of Owen Sound. Beaches, meadows, shorelines all around us, the Niagara Escarpment, forests, small towns to big cities. It's all within reach."

Greg has taken his knowledge of iPhone photography and begun doing speaking engagements in his local area and hopes someday to eventually have the opportunity to speak at larger conferences.

More of Greg's photography can be seen on Instagram @mcmillanphoto, on Glass @greg, or on his website at mcmillan.photos.

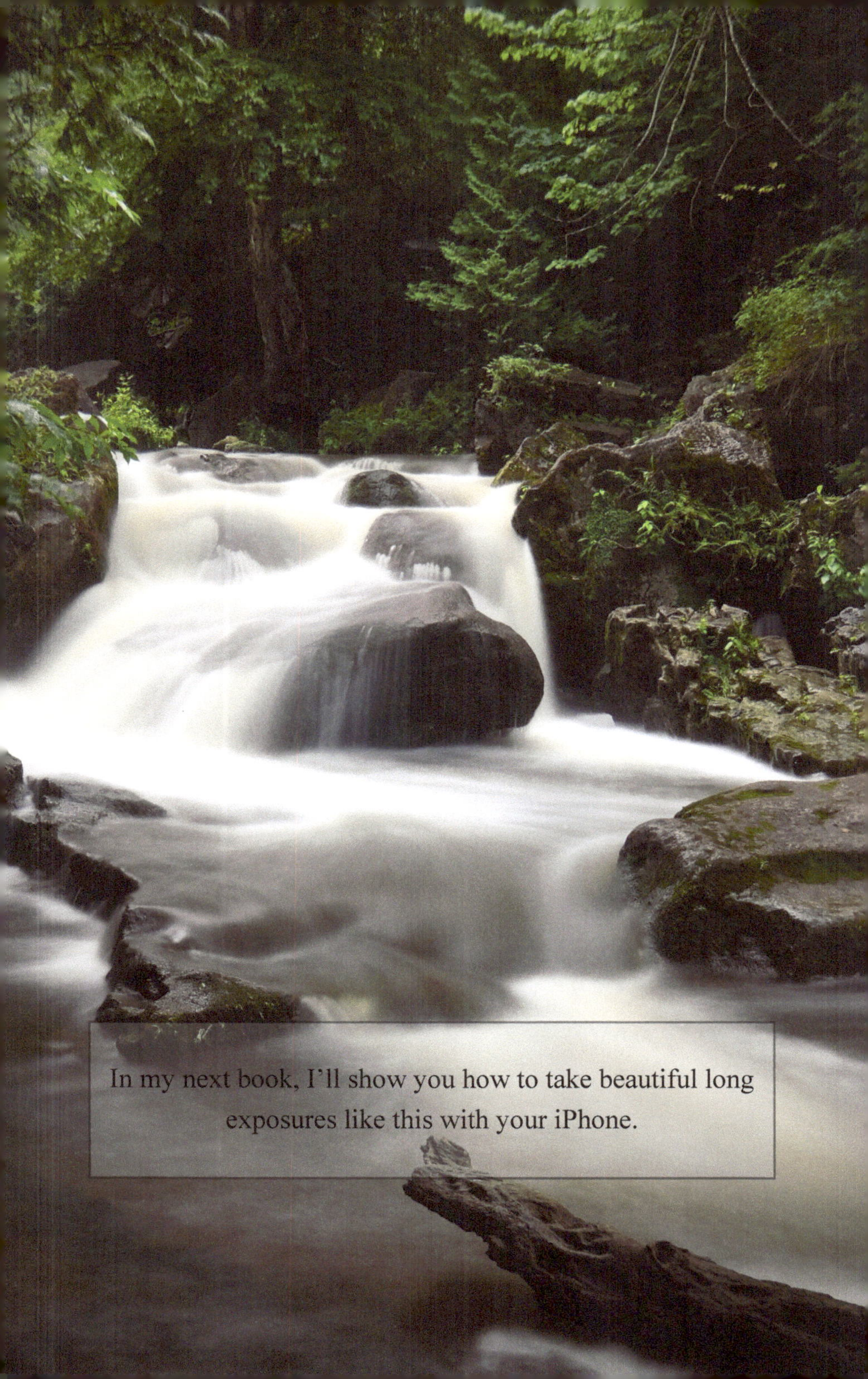

In my next book, I'll show you how to take beautiful long exposures like this with your iPhone.